D1220180

Getting Home

How one question started our journey
of continuous improvement

by

Liz McCartney
Zack Rosenburg

with
Emily Adams

Published by the Lean Enterprise Institute, Inc.

Lean Enterprise Institute

Book design: Thomas Skehan; Cover design: Mark Karis
Library of Congress Control Number: 2019935925
ISBN: 978-1-934109-56-4

Lean Enterprise Institute, Inc.
27–43 Wormwood Street
Tower Point, Suite 401, Boston, MA 02210
617-871-2900 • fax: 617-871-2999 • lean.org

This book is dedicated to the hundreds of thousands of volunteers, donors, staff, and AmeriCorps members who selflessly help people they have never met before who, after disaster, are at risk of being pushed beyond their breaking point.

blank

CONTENTS

FOREWORD

There is plenty of room for innovation in every walk of life, such as inventing a hydrogen fuel-cell car that emits only water vapor and zero emissions. Or developing a robot with enough finger dexterity to play the trumpet and, more importantly, perform basic tasks for the elderly and disabled.

At Toyota, we're proud of these technological advances and so many others our global company has created since 1937. But, for every innovative idea, we knew we could not do it alone. So we partner with like-minded innovators such as SBP. This nonprofit possesses the heart, dedication, and can-do spirit to rebuild homes for the most desperate Americans after a disaster. But SBP wanted to do more and improve its processes to help more families and make rebuilding go *faster*.

SBP and Toyota understand that the importance of communities recovering quickly can have a profound impact on people. Toyota has been a part of the cultural fabric in the United States and North America for more than 60 years; it was a natural fit for us to help support the great work of SBP.

Initially, SBP asked for monetary donations. While our support includes money, we also provide a fleet of Toyota trucks, our team members give their time to volunteer, and we connect SBP to other business partners.

But perhaps the most meaningful contribution from Toyota was to share something that SBP and hundreds of other nonprofits now consider to be just as valuable as money—the Toyota Production System (TPS), which helps deliver the best quality, lowest cost, and shortest lead time through the elimination of waste.

In these pages, you will read about and be inspired by the spirit of a defense lawyer and a school teacher who left their careers to rebuild homes for the most desperate survivors of Hurricane Katrina in New Orleans. What Liz McCartney and Zack Rosenburg quickly discovered about this work is that the duration of time between disaster and recovery inflicts an immense toll on people. They were determined to do better, and Toyota wanted to help.

By sharing the Toyota Production System with SBP, we helped reduce home-rebuilding time by about 50%. SBP applied what it has learned about process improvement and increased the capabilities of its entire organization. Toyota is pleased that SBP is now sharing its TPS knowledge with others to help rebuild homes and lives following disasters throughout the US and its territories.

As root cause problem-solvers steeped in the Toyota Production System, SBP is also working hard to mitigate the impact of a disaster *before* it even hits, by training people to be properly prepared for storms that can happen. At Toyota, this spirit of continuous improvement is what we call innovation.

We hope you enjoy this firsthand account of the SBP journey.

Jim Lentz, CEO
Toyota Motor North America, Inc.

blank

A Teacher and a Lawyer
Walk into a Hippie Tent

The eeriest thing was the stillness. Especially at night when there should have been bugs and frogs singing all around, we would lie in our tent and listen to the silence. There were no birds to wake us up in the morning, only the sounds of people wrestling pots and pans, preparing breakfast. In the middle of a once-vibrant parish just outside New Orleans proper, it was too quiet.

This was six months after Hurricane Katrina hit the Gulf Coast, six months after the levees failed and stormwater rushed through streets, over and into homes, businesses, and hospitals. New Orleans filled up like a bowl. The water fast became a toxic stew of lake water, industrial runoff, fossil fuels, and sewage. Over Labor Day weekend 2005, from our home in Washington, DC, we watched news coverage in horror as people were rescued—or worse, waited to be rescued—off rooftops and trees, dazed and sunburned, while dead bodies and cars floated down neighborhood streets.

Six months after the storm, we—Liz McCartney, middle-school teacher and executive director of a technology learning lab, and Zack Rosenburg, criminal defense lawyer for the indigent—still had those images seared into our brains, and we felt like we had to do something. Liz emailed 20 groups involved in the recovery effort, offering our help, and heard back from just one. We made plans to take a short leave from our jobs and our lives to go do whatever we could. It was a decision that would upend our lives and our ideas about what was possible or practical.

As it turns out, helping people recover from a disaster is both easier and far more complicated than we could have ever imagined. And yet, like any human endeavor, recovery is a series of processes that can be improved or radically reimagined to better serve people. But first, we had to find out what we did not know.

Liz went first. During the 17-hour drive down to Louisiana, she second-guessed our decision. She wasn't afraid of hard work. But the storm was six months past, and the national news had largely moved on. An Egyptian passenger ferry had sunk in the Red Sea, killing more than 1,000 people. The Winter Olympics were about to begin in Turin, Italy. Sometimes there were reports about trouble with response of the Federal Emergency Management Agency (FEMA) in the hurricane's path, but the major coverage seemed to be winding down. After all, 19 of her emails had gone unanswered. Liz wondered whether help was still needed.

She pulled into the city after dark and went straight to her hotel in the French Quarter. The narrow brick streets had been spared the flood, but bars and restaurants were still subdued. Liz saw a tree uprooted and lying across a sidewalk, which was odd. Surely that was the kind of storm damage that would have been cleared away months ago. Had something else happened more recently?

Early the next morning, she started across town to the relief organization and immediately came across a massive fire burning on St. Claude Avenue, forcing her to redirect through neighborhoods she did not know. From the Upper Ninth Ward and across the Industrial Canal to the Lower Ninth Ward, block after block of utter ruin slipped past her windshield. There were cars on top of houses and houses on top of cars. One house was splayed open, split like a piece of overripe fruit, with personal possessions spilling toward the street and flapping in the light breeze.

There were endless piles of debris in front of houses, in vacant lots, and at the ends of streets as if pushed there by a snowplow. Much of it was covered with a kind of thick, furry blanket. The blanket consisted of shredded clothes, splintered wood, insulation, and who knows what else, all fused together with mildew that had dried out and rewetted with every passing rain for half a year. Long-existing landmarks had disappeared under this furry camouflage. New landmarks appeared: a 30-foot fishing boat resting on its side in a residential neighborhood; a house in the Lower Ninth Ward with all its walls, roof, and furniture blown out and washed away—all that remained was a lone toilet on a cement slab.

Liz kept driving east along the north shore of the Mississippi River until she reached Chalmette, where a few relief organizations had set up tents to help feed the storm refugees, providing food to areas without operating grocery stores or restaurants. Chalmette is the parish seat of St. Bernard Parish, home to 60,000 people (pre-flood). Six months after the storm, there were just five businesses open: a gas station, a car wash, a hair salon, a barbershop, and a local bar. In the middle, there were a few clusters of big tents that made up the odd collection of relief efforts.

There was the Blackwater complex run by the federal government's security contractors, best known for providing extra armed personnel for the conflicts in Iraq and Afghanistan. After Katrina passed through, Blackwater forces were hired for private security jobs. Then the company secured a contract offering relief services. To get into its tented compound, you had to pass through metal detectors and pat-down searches. People looking for a hot meal had to leave their oyster knives outside.

Nearby was the religious tent. This was staffed by people from all over the country, organized by their churches back home to spend a week or two in New Orleans, to help feed and comfort people wounded by tragedy.

And then there was what everyone called the hippie tent, organized by people affiliated with the Rainbow Family. It is an understatement to say that the people staffing this giant, geodesic, dome-like structure were eclectic. There were hippies in flowing skirts and beards, working class tradespeople, and suburban soccer moms all serving side-by-side. A man with an eye patch worked beside college kids and recently returned veterans, because everyone was just there to help.

Outside of New Orleans, the Rainbow Family was best known for holding enormous annual gatherings in national parks devoted to meditations for peace and wild dancing, exploring new-age ideas and psychedelics. They had no leaders or spokespeople or official organizational structure, yet they held these summer gatherings every year that lasted about a month and attracted 10,000–20,000 people. Employees of the National Park Service have said that when this gathering—the size of a small city—left a campground, you could not tell that they had been there.

Over the years, Rainbow Family members had developed some expertise in cooking for masses of people, setting up mobile kitchens and health clinics, and creating both supply and distribution networks. They put those skills to use in New Orleans, setting up camps in Chalmette and Marigny, often teaming up with religious groups to make use of uneven resources. They did such a good job that the United Way agreed to fund their efforts, and so, six months after the storm, the Rainbow Family was still there, putting out three hot, delicious meals a day—usually bean intensive—fueled by volunteers who camped out behind the makeshift kitchen. That was where Liz pitched her tent.

After a week, Zack joined Liz in the tent. And then Liz's newly retired mother, Marion McCartney, came down and pitched a tent beside ours. Our days fell into a simple rhythm, rising at 5 a.m. to help in the kitchen, serving meals to people, and then sitting with them and talking. They came to the hippie tent for food but also to be surrounded by something other than FEMA trailers and damaged or gutted homes. People needed a spark of humanity and to connect with others.

Some people were shell-shocked and quiet. But most wanted to talk, to tell their stories in order to preserve their identities. These were people who had built their own lives, done for themselves, and been productive members of St. Bernard Parish or the Ninth Ward before Katrina whipped through and took so much away. We cannot recall a single person asking for help. They told stories, traded updates on family members and neighbors, and passed along any information they had on FEMA activities and rebuilding efforts.

We made friends and were invited into people's homes. We stood in gutted shells and, more frequently, in homes not yet gutted where you could still see a thick band of black mold growing up the living room wall, crawling over family photos to the high-water line. To take the place of missing and damaged roofs, FEMA had distributed tens of thousands of huge blue tarps to homeowners, so most of our conversations took place in this watery blue light in sagging rooms filled with the stench of mold and whatever else the black water had left behind.

We talked about rebuilding and about family. Contractors were hard to find, and not all of them were honest. Lots of people did not have enough or the right kind of insurance. Often, if they had insurance against water damage, their claims would get turned down because inspectors said the damage was due to wind. Sometimes it was the other way around.

Beyond the destruction and loss, we began hearing another common story. People were suffering because Katrina had dismantled their support networks. Nearly everyone we met had grown up in St. Bernard Parish or the City of New Orleans and lived within a few blocks of family. Before, when bad or challenging things happened, people turned to a sibling or aunt or cousins or in-laws. But now those homes were destroyed too, and people had fled to Baton Rogue or Houston. The people still in the parish or New Orleans six months after the storm were often alone for the first time in their lives.

Like Mr. Andre. We first met Mr. Andre in the hippie tent, where he was a regular. A very tall man, Mr. Andre had the kind of proud bearing that made you forget about the walker that he used to get from the food line to the communal tables. He would wave off any offers to help carry his food tray but was happy to sit and chat about his family, his career, and his community before the storm. He was at the hippie tent for every single meal.

Mr. Andre was a veteran of WWII and wore one of those trucker hats with a padded front and mesh back; his service pins and medals adorned the front. When he came home from Germany after the war, he found a job as a steel worker and made a good living. He married, sent his children to college, and paid off his house. He did not have insurance because he did not live in a mandatory flood insurance zone—there was "no need."

Long after the dinner service wrapped up, he would sit at one of the tables drinking coffee and chatting. More often than not, one of us would join him just for the pleasure of his company in those long, quiet nights before we crawled into our cold tents and sleeping bags.

Early one morning, we walked into the meal tent and saw Mr. Andre sobbing. His shoulders shaking over a cup of coffee at his usual table, he finally choked out a few words. It was this painful,

Walk into a Hippie Tent

predictable routine that finally got to him, he said, with no end in sight. Every morning he had breakfast with us at the hippie tent. Then he got into his blue Ford Ranger pickup truck, drove over to the FEMA office, and waited in line to ask for a trailer to live in. A clerk would tell him there were no trailers, and he would leave there and come back to have lunch with us. After lunch, he would go back to FEMA and wait in the same line. He asked the same question and got the same answer.

Mr. Andre ate dinner late and spent long hours lingering at the table. He was always one of the last to leave, and we wondered why. On that sad morning we discovered the answer. Each night he delayed the moment when he would drive back to the FEMA lot and try to sleep in the back of his truck. That was how he had been living for three months.

Mr. Andre was in his mid- or late 80s. His back bowed when he was tired, and his hands shook sometimes. That morning, he told us through his tears about Germany, where he had served just after WWII ended. So many people there were living in abject poverty, scrapping together supplies for bread and soup in bombed-out cities. But the worst part, they told him, was that they felt forgotten. The world had moved on and abandoned them to their fates with no clear path forward. Mr. Andre finally understood what that meant, to be in misery and forgotten.

Burrowed deep into our sleeping bags that night, we agonized over what we could do to help him and wondered how many more Mr. Andres there were out there.

Days later, we finally gave in to our own physical discomfort and got a hotel room for the night, giving Marion the hot shower she had been yearning for. While she went to bed early, we took a walk through the French Quarter and Marginy. Our time was nearly up, but we were having a hard time thinking about going back to

DC. We loved our lives there; we each had work that was important and fulfilling. But there was an immediate, unmet, and profoundly human need in Louisiana.

Finally it was Zack who said, "We have to come back and do something. We can't just leave." Liz listed a series of concerns, but her heart was not in any pushback. A day later, we committed.

Of course, we were imagining something rational, like finding a more substantial way to help and spending a year in New Orleans. We started talking to people. In the Katrina disaster zone, you got to know the real power brokers pretty quickly. We had already met most of them. So we found the local leaders of national organizations and on-the-ground FEMA representatives and asked, "What's the plan? What's the next step in rebuilding?"

The plan, we heard, was first to gut all the houses. In an operation that would last more than a year, teams of people would move through—house after block after parish—and systematically gut one house after another. So a block that got gutted at the beginning of the effort would just sit there, until the last house was gutted a dozen miles away. We were repeatedly told that this is how recovery had been done for 30 years. Why change? Rebuilding was phase three and could not be started until after phases one and two were done.

While we may not have recognized it at the time, this was our first introduction to the human toll and systematic inefficiency that occur when fidelity to process outweighs measuring what matters. We saw a system designed in theory for success; unfortunately, success was defined by following a process, not achieving results that matter to people.

It is difficult, still, to imagine the scale of the destruction caused by Hurricane Katrina. Eighty percent of New Orleans was underwater in the days after the storm; 1,577 people died. In St. Bernard Parish, the municipality that includes Chalmette, 95% of the housing units were damaged, equaling more than 25,000 homes.

At the time, we knew nothing about the difference between batch-versus-flow operations, but we knew instinctively that first gutting every last house was wrong. We had talked to enough people and spent time on enough blocks to know that places did not come back to life until someone returned home. People might drive past their old house to look, but they did not stop unless they saw a neighbor, some human activity, and a reason to justify their hopes.

We believed that we could make a big difference in the time line, but we were not entirely sure where to put our energies first. So, we went home to DC and held a fundraiser while we made plans. A few weeks later, Mr. Andre called to report that he was finally getting his FEMA trailer delivered to the front of his ruined house.

We continued packing up our apartment and arranged to be absent from our jobs for extended periods.

Mr. Andre called again, this time weakened and in despair. After a couple of weeks in the FEMA trailer, for which he had no keys, he had terrible diarrhea and the toilet was backed up. We made some calls on his behalf and felt an even deeper urge to be on the ground as soon as possible.

Finally, with a minivan full of donated and borrowed tools—most of which we did not know how to use—we returned to New Orleans on June 1, 2006 to set up shop.

We found our first clients, Joey and Melody Ladapie, on referral from George Barasich, head of the local fishermen's union, whom we had met in the hippie tent. We got volunteers from Craigslist, walked into the Ladapies' 1,300-square-foot brick ranch house in St. Bernard Parish, and felt a pang of doubt. We did not really know what we were doing. But they needed help and we were determined.

The house had already been gutted, so we got to work cutting and hanging Sheetrock on the bare framing. Over the next few weeks, we screwed in drywall, applied a layer of mud over it,[1] and painted every wall and ceiling. When we were done, the Ladapies thanked us profusely and then said, "Go to the next family. We'll take it from here."

Seeing the confidence in their faces, we saw our path. We wrote up a business plan showing that with $50,000, we could install new Sheetrock walls and ceilings, all painted, for 20 families. Based on that plan, Gary Ostroske, the CEO of the United Way of Southeast Louisiana, took a chance and funded our efforts.

We started out doing one house at a time, adding in plumbing and electrical work as needed. But we were inundated with requests for help and quickly moved to have several sites running at the same time. How best to do that is a challenge we have been solving and re-solving ever since.

Still, there were more clients—more people like Mr. Andre whose health and prospects became more fragile the longer they lived in precarious situations with no clear path home. For too many people, running between service agencies, insurers, and government agencies trying to coordinate money and construction help was a frustrating full-time job.

So we created an all-under-one-roof model where clients would not have to run from one agency to the next, learning how to apply for all kinds of government-sponsored aid. Though relatively small-

---

1. Also known as joint compound, this is the layer that gives walls the plaster-like texture while protecting the underlying Sheetrock.

scale, we focused on giving clients predictability, reliability, and, perhaps most important, a central point of contact. We recruited volunteers, performed case management, raised funds, did construction, and pulled permits on our clients' behalf.

Clients now had a one-stop shop. We became better at hiring and managing plumbers, electricians, HVAC contractors, and roofers; at eradicating mold, efficiently applying mud to drywall, and finding corporate sponsorship. We tapped into sources for volunteers and learned to manage all that casual labor and keep it coordinated with the tradespeople. With essential support from AmeriCorps, thousands of volunteers from across the country, and sponsorship from Entergy, Shell, United Way, and many generous individuals, St. Bernard Project—SBP—was born.

By October 2007, 16 months after arriving in town with our borrowed tools, we had celebrated homecomings for 88 families. Meanwhile, the official Long-Term Recovery Committee—in which separate groups handled case management, fundraising, gutting, rebuilding, and volunteer coordination—had managed to secure funding to begin rebuilding on only 13 homes. We became convinced we had found the right way to help people.

Mr. Andre finally made it out of his FEMA trailer and into his house with help from other contractors. But sadly, he seemed to lose his spirit. He died not long after getting home.

Those first years were filled with wild highs and lows. We found incredibly passionate and committed people to populate our tiny staff, along with big reserves of volunteer labor. We found fellow Americans who were compelled by citizenship and compassion to travel sometimes-long distances to help total strangers. Some were tradespeople who had left their jobs; others were grandparents or professional athletes. All these people were willing to sweat, haul, and build. We were inspired every day by their hard work and commitment. A pair of students at Loyola University organized their friends to hang Sheetrock on so many weekends that they finally made it official and became the Loyola Shrocking Club. We also found an amazing partnership with AmeriCorps, the federally funded agency that attracts people from all walks of life to improve lives for other Americans.

Sometimes, 30 volunteers would show up on a rainy Saturday to work on a 900-square-foot house. Other times, we worked alone. If one staff person left, we scrambled to fill the gap but lost all the knowledge and skill that person had gained throughout their tenure.

Our numbers improved over time, going from 88 homecomings in 16 months to 100 or more a year. Some houses took far longer than we thought they would or should. We knew we had problems with construction and coordination, but we could not quite identify exactly what those problems were. The questions became urgent when deadlines got pushed and clients' faces dropped in anguish.

Finally, a member of our board of directors offered to introduce us to a very knowledgeable local building consultant. Maybe he could help us improve. We eagerly jumped on the offer and gave this expert a tour of our offices, warehouse, and field operations.

In the world of charity work, it can be difficult to find truth-tellers. People were quick to applaud our efforts and our resilience. It was hard for them to understand that we were not looking for applause and "participant" awards. We judged ourselves by the families we helped and the rate of still-pressing need.

This man seemed to understand that, and we are still grateful for his candor. He sat us down, spread his hands on the table and said, "You're a mess."

Are You Ahead or Behind?
SBP Meets TPS

By this point, we at the St. Bernard Project had been mucking out and rebuilding homes for about five years. We had blown right past our original one-year commitment when we realized the recovery was not even close to halfway complete. By 2011 we had welcomed home more than 400 families and learned a lot about construction. But we still had a waiting list of hundreds of families in the parish and, having expanded into New Orleans, a citywide need in the tens of thousands.

Five years after Katrina, people were still living in homes full of mold, with rotten floors, and sometimes without electricity. Hard-working families were living in gutted homes and sheds, sleeping on bare plywood or on relatives' couches in far-flung cities, wondering whether they would ever get home. Depression was common. Many blocks were still half empty and too quiet.

Added to that, we were clearly coming to the end of an era of norms. In the first few years of rebuilding, our clients were unique, but the construction jobs were pretty similar, repairing storm damage to comparable houses in the St. Bernard Parish. These were mostly three bedroom, two bath, slab-on-grade, single-story, brick-facade homes of less than 1,300 square feet. Most houses were already gutted, and we could see what was needed pretty easily. After all, we had worked on hundreds of houses just like these.

Now our inputs were changing. We were working more often in New Orleans, on houses that were vastly different—one from the other—and most held secrets. Open up the kitchen wall on a

90-year-old wood-frame house, particularly one that has already suffered some repairs by a homeowner in the 1960s and then a shady contractor in 2006, and an entire construction schedule could get thrown out the window. Workdays too often felt like barely controlled chaos.

While we readily accepted the idea that our methods had room for improvement, we had plenty of distractions. We started new programs, such as Good Work/Good Pay that offered a living wage to veterans returning from wars in Iraq and Afghanistan and taught them the building trades by our licensed plumbers, electricians, and builders. And we focused on building a great training environment for our young staff.

Then a kind soul donated three empty lots in the Ninth Ward so that we could build affordable housing. We started our first ground-up construction projects and experimented with prefab construction and new materials. We had lots of optimism and enthusiasm. What we did not have was a clear, workable path to improve our "mess."

And that's when we met Toyota. The then-head of Toyota USA Foundation, Patricia Pineda, heard us give a public presentation about our work. Seated with Pat at dinner afterward, Liz shared her frustrations with the slow pace of recovery. Pat listened patiently and then asked Liz whether she had heard of the Toyota Production System (TPS) and its method of removing wasted time and resources from processes. It was a conversation that would forever change us, SBP, and our ideas of what is possible in the aftermath of disaster.

Pat helped us enlist Toyota as a corporate partner and set up an interview for us with the Toyota Production System Support Center (TSSC). TSSC is a not-for-profit organization dedicated to helping manufacturers, government entities, and nonprofits like SBP reduce waste and increase efficiency by utilizing TPS. We learned that TPS is not just a set of tools but an integrated management system and philosophy that, though an uncomfortable fit for us at first, in time became inseparable from the way that we view the world.

Initially, via phone interviews, leaders from TSSC assessed our leadership to make sure we could—and would—commit to making real change. Then, they agreed to come to Louisiana and take a closer look.

So, the global players, the big boys, were going to come to our industrial-park offices in Chalmette to look at what we were doing and tell us the secrets to making things work on a grand scale. It was equally exciting and unnerving. Zack remembers his nerves. Would SBP even be sophisticated enough to warrant a return visit?

Mark Reich, general manager of TSSC, came to SBP headquarters for our initial evaluation. Tall and with a serious disposition (to Zack's mind, anyway), Mark sat in on our morning meeting with leads from construction and plumbing, electricians, volunteer coordinators, and client services. Our conference room, which doubled as Zack's office, was not large, and there were boxes and stacks of paper piled all around. The walls were covered with pictures, notices, and drawings from our clients' children.

Mark sat with us at the cramped table and listened as we went around and talked about what the staff and tradespeople were doing that day. Our lead plumber and his crew were doing an initial evaluation at one house, a rough-in of pipes on two houses, and fixing some mistakes on another. The lead electrician cited a similar work schedule, and our volunteer coordinator talked about the number of volunteers we had painting and hanging drywall in houses. At the very least, we thought Mark could see how carefully we were managing our resources.

Then Mark said he had a question and asked us, "Do you talk about problems?"

Zack nodded enthusiastically. "Absolutely," he said out loud, nodding and smiling, and then looking around the table and noticing that everyone else was shaking their heads *no* and looking askance. It is doubtful that we even had a common definition of the word *problem*. If Mark told us he meant any deviation from the standard, we would have had to ask what he meant by *standard*. This was not the kind of language we used.

Mark turned to Liz and asked, "Are you ahead or behind?"

"Of what?" Liz asked.

"Ahead or behind on your schedule, goals, or expectations?"

The truth is we did not know. We did not set firm schedules. People in the building trades were fond of saying that, with old houses especially, there were too many unknowns to set a time line. We accepted this judgment because we were newcomers to the field and still learning. It didn't seem right to us, but what did we know?

Mark also wondered how we managed our client expectations. The truth again, we did not do a very good job of it. We told our clients, "We're working as fast as we can." But we could not tell them with any real certainty when they might move home.

Mark spent the rest of the day going to job sites, touring our warehouse, and talking with site supervisors and tradespeople. When he was done, he told us that he could see two things: 1) we passionately wanted to improve, and that was more than half the battle, but 2) most of our problems centered on the fact that we were not truly client-focused.

This was astonishing. It hurt.

We had abandoned our careers, moved away from family, and dedicated our lives and energy to helping people recover from disaster. And yet, our organization was not oriented to the client?

Mark went back to Kentucky to discuss our case with his team, while we were left wondering what they might suggest. Our first TSSC advisor, Brian Bichey, arrived with a mandate to turn SBP's focus to the client. Like Mark, he spent the first day observing us.

In 2011, we had a staff of about 41—most of them tradespeople, construction coordinators, a small fundraising staff, and a handful of people leading the departments. In addition, we were granted the ability to recruit and hire about 40 AmeriCorps members every year. These are American citizens from across the country, often young people a few years out of college, who agree to work for the benefit of others for 10 months of their lives, earning stipends of about $1,100 a month while working their tails off. We are in collective awe of the AmeriCorps members who have come through our organization. Many of our staff are former AmeriCorps members. They all start out as direct-impact workers: as job-site supervisors, in warehouse and supply, or in client services.

A few of our amazing AmeriCorps members.

At the very front line—what manufacturers might call touch labor—we had volunteers: groups from service clubs, companies big and small, families, schools on spring break, church groups, and others who joined us to work for a week or a day. At the beginning of volunteer shifts, they received a little training from the AmeriCorps site supervisor, and then, no matter the skill level they came in with, they spent the day hanging drywall, applying mud to the drywall, sanding, painting, tiling floors, installing insulation—whatever needed to be done.

To understand how we worked, Brian enlisted Liz to help build a process map. Using emails, time sheets, and memory, they used the experiences we had at a couple of recent jobs and retraced every step made by staff and volunteers to rebuild a house. They found most strikingly that we did a lot of fixing. Time after time, our people went back over the same rooms, the same plumbing or roofing or windows, fixing work that was not up to code or was just not right.

A group of volunteers ready to work.

Our people did not make a big deal out of this. They did not complain loudly or even talk much about mistakes. Everyone knew our Grandparent Rule: if the work was not good enough for your own grandparents or loved ones, it was not right. Our people were accustomed to fixing issues without fanfare.

In 2011, it took us an average of 116 days to complete a house. We worked on 15–30 houses concurrently, so our annual rate of completion was not terrible, but we knew it could be better. We wanted it to be a lot better.

We were prepared for Brian to tell us that we needed to work smarter, or maybe just faster. What he suggested, however, seemed a little nutty. He said we could improve our lead time on a house—how much time it takes to complete the job—by changing the focus of our morning meeting. Instead of asking what the plumbers or electricians were doing, we needed to ask whether we were ahead or behind schedule on the Hendersons' house. Then we should move on to talking about the Smiths' and the Freemans' houses.

If we had a clear time frame for when the work *should* be done, and if every morning we asked whether we were sending the right resources—people, expertise, materials, and tools—to the job site to get the work completed on schedule, we could cut our lead time in half. In. Half.

"This was all pretty new to SBP. I don't think people realized how much waiting and waste there really was," Brian says.

Before joining TSSC, Brian had managed the plastics shop for Toyota Motor Corp. in Indiana, where they build the Tundra and Sequoia models. He was a mechanical engineer. We knew that he had knowledge that a couple of liberal arts majors like us did not. Still, if he had not been so disarmingly positive, we would have had a very hard time hearing his message. It just seemed so unlikely.

The first thing we needed, he said, was a big whiteboard where we could write all the necessary information and see our work. This would be the focal point for all of our morning meetings. Instead of listening (or not) to one verbal progress report after another, we would virtually look at each job site, what it needed, and whether it was running on track. We could finally answer one of Mark's two questions: we would know whether we were ahead or behind.

Enlisting Liz's help, Brian got a couple of dry-erase boards and did test runs in the morning meeting, making sure he understood everything the team needed to know about the job sites. Then he and Liz went to just about every automotive parts store in St. Bernard Parish and bought rolls and rolls of black pinstriping tape. With pinstripe tape, they created dozens of rows—each row represented a family's home, capturing years of worry and heartache. Vertical columns were created to show specific phases of construction that needed to get done: plumbing, electrical, flooring, framing, mudding, paint, etc. (see right).

When a house went up on the board, the columns to the right were filled with abbreviations for the work to be done on particular dates. If the work was not done by the target date, we would ask why. This would bring problems to the surface to be cataloged and put on a separate rework board to analyze the data. Which phases had the most problems, and within those phases, what were the most common problems? When we found problems repeating, we would go to the source and observe the situation.

This sounds pretty straightforward, but remember that when Mark asked whether we discussed problems, only Zack believed that we did. Now, we were supposed to stand at this board every morning and openly discuss any problems that we might have meeting our clients' needs.

Our original pinstriped production boards.

For us, it quickly became clear that we did not have a good system for scheduling the trades and checking their work. There was a lot of rework happening because we did not have clearly stated standards for what finished work should look like and, to be fair, tradespeople were often being jerked from one job to the next.

Some of this we tried to excuse as the nature of our work. Construction does not always follow a linear path, especially on our jobs. In any one house, we might be juggling tile work in one room and hanging doors and trim in the next. General contractors do not schedule work like this, but we have to make use of volunteers as we get them. A bit of chaotic opportunism is always with us.

Brian pointed out that there are many situations that repeat time and again on job sites. We always need to run electrical wires, install outlets, hang drywall, and find the roughed-in electrical outlets. He suggested that we use our most skilled workers to take dissimilar houses to a constant state. Then volunteers—the lowest skilled—

A close up of a recent production board.

could have simple, repeatable tasks. This meant that the work of our tradespeople could be mapped out and we could understand how long it should take to complete various pieces of a job. Once we understood the vision of having our tradespeople do more standardized work within clear time lines, we would have to be fully committed to using the crazy pinstriped boards, just to know whether we were ahead or behind.

Every. Single. Day.

And we needed that daily commitment because there was a fair amount of resistance to standing there every morning and asking people questions like, "Did that task get finished? Why not? When will you be ready to move on to the Hendersons' house?"

From a collection of well-meaning heroes, and with some pretty ad hoc work methods, we were asking the organization to become more predictable and accountable. We were asking people *when* the work would be finished and *why* didn't it happen yesterday.

A daily meeting in front of the production board.

We were trying to understand the nature of our problems, not blaming people. Still, buried resentments come up pretty quick when you start talking about problems. Liz had to step into the middle of a couple of arguments that verged on fistfights.

We learned to stop asking questions like, "Did you finish that job?" that were just too aggressive and, more importantly, too vague. Instead, we learned to ask about progress on components. For instance, if a kitchen needs to be replaced, plumbers and electricians begin with a rough-in phase, running hot and cold water pipes or electrical cables along routes inside walls and anchoring them in place. Then they withdraw until walls and cabinets are put in place and then return for the finish phase of installing sinks, outlets, etc.

We found that asking, "Will the Smith house be ready for cabinets tomorrow?" was a lot more palatable than asking Joe whether his team was done. Over time, we even began to ask questions like, "What does success look like?" and to make sure that we were aligned on the definition of success.

After working with us twice a month for about six months, Brian left to bring improvement to a school district in Massachusetts. The next person from TSSC was another mechanical engineer, Sylvester DuPree. He came in with an idea that had seemed near impossible to us before: *standardization.*

Sylvester understood from his years of experience at Toyota that every process could be standardized and then improved. He wanted to begin with the plumbers. We tried not to be pessimistic, even though we had listened for years to plumbers describing their work as utterly unpredictable. He spent long days studying the plumbers and their workflows. He looked for repeated action and for best practices and talked to the plumbers about the way they preferred to work. Soon, he identified standardization's ground zero: the plumbing rough-in.

Because just about every job begins by installing the initial water and sewer lines into the framing of a house, this piece of work dictated when everything else could begin. In studying the work, Sylvester saw that there was a lot of predictability to it. When done right, running hot and cold water lines from source to tap looks pretty much the same in every house. There really is not a whole lot of creative interpretation or free-styling that should happen here.

Sylvester proposed that apprentice plumbers could be trained to do a standardized plumbing rough-in, leaving the master plumber free to move among job sites, checking work, answering questions, and performing more specialized tasks.

It made perfect sense. With the work broken down into component steps and realistic time lines, we could talk more clearly about what was needed to complete the work and how we might support both the job and the schedule.

This was a revelation.

Joplin, Missouri

This was not the only way SBP was changing. On the evening of May 22, 2011, a tornado struck Joplin, Missouri, tearing up a mile-wide swath of the town, killing 158 people, injuring 1,150, and destroying 6,954 homes. Another 359 homes had major damage. Watching the news coverage of people searching for loved ones and pieces of their homes brought back those early despondent months after Hurricane Katrina. Only now, we were better prepared to help.

We sent Zack to Joplin to see whether they needed our assistance. Then we sent a team to assess needs and assist in early relief efforts. They worked at gutting houses and client outreach by day and slept in church pews at night. Sylvester went too, in order to help us identify the standardized work to disaster response.

Zack created a partnership with another relief organization, Rebuild Joplin. Rebuild Joplin leaders reminded us of ourselves five years earlier, just with different accents and a kinder disposition. They were outsiders to the disaster recovery ecosystem, compelled by an inner calling to leave the sidelines to ensure that their community was rebuilt. Jerrod Hogan and his team of civic leaders opened our eyes to two things.

First, we learned that an unpredictable path forward after a disaster is something that is faced by smaller communities in smaller disasters. Second, we learned that in communities across America, there are people who will rally to help and who are also searching for a path that measures real success, not just fidelity to a process. The eventually successful recovery in Joplin, hard won by the government, business, civic, faith-based, and NGO groups,[2] became a teaching moment for SBP. We knew we could no longer view success as limited by the boundaries of New Orleans.

One other note: while tens of thousands of volunteers and dozens of corporations supported the recovery, one corporation played an indelible role. Jeff Dailey, the CEO of Farmers Insurance, got wind of SBP's work in Joplin. A visionary leader committed to innovation and impact who has fierce pride in his team, Jeff invested Farmers' best asset—their people—in the recovery. For one year, Farmers sent employees every day to rebuild houses, agreeing to stop only when the recovery was complete. Farmers' investment gave the physical and emotional push that allowed the recovery to be successfully completed.

---

2. Nongovernment organizations (NGOs) are usually nonprofit groups that can have a wide variety of missions.

In 2012, we began rebuilding houses for people in Joplin. As in Louisiana, we focused on the elderly, handicapped, and families with young children, most of whom were either uninsured or denied coverage. Our construction teams spent 18 months there—until our house-by-house survey told us that rebuilding was complete. We rebuilt 181 homes and learned a lot about how to respond better and more quickly to disasters.

Meanwhile, back in New Orleans, our morning talks about problems had highlighted issues in the warehouse. This is where we store everything from ladders and drills, to paint, caulk, mud, and drywall screws left over from one house and waiting to be used on another. Our warehouse and supply coordinators deliver tools and materials to job sites, do the shopping at home improvement centers and lumber yards, and track costs per job site.

It's a big job. Supply coordinators spent a lot of time searching though piles of cast-off materials in our warehouse, looking for a box of tools or supplies to deliver to a job site. Some material became obsolete or expired on the shelves, or supplies piled up because we purchased too much or forgot what we had.

Sylvester helped pull together a cross-functional improvement team and taught us the 5S principles: sort, straighten, shine, standardize, and sustain. Our warehouse manager increased 5S to six, with the addition of *safety*. It was a lot like doing a massive clean-and-organize operation on your garage, if you were a home-improvement hoarder. Within a week, we had all the ladders stacked together in a clearly labeled spot for ladders. Paint, caulk, and screws occupied clearly labeled shelves. Electric drills and saws—which had a tendency to wander—got a new home in a locked cage with its own checkout sheet.

More importantly, we standardized the supply request forms based on different phases of construction. Project managers use these sheets to make sure job sites have the necessary tools and materials based on the work that is happening and the number of volunteers. We never want a dozen volunteers trying to paint a house with one ladder and five paintbrushes. So, project managers give these requests to supply coordinators who deliver everything to the job sites.

Every time we gutted a storm-damaged house, for instance, we needed safety glasses, respirator masks to protect against mold and lead-based paint, work gloves, utility knives, and lots of utility blades. Why write it down every time? We realized that, if we had a lot of houses to gut, we could make gutting kit boxes. Likewise, we could create electrical rough-in kits, plumbing finish preorder forms, and drywall templates.

Banks of ladders in clearly marked spots.

Instead of painstakingly writing out every order with all of those duplications, our supply coordinators could pull up standardized lists, do a couple of additions or deletions if necessary, and have extra time to organize materials and talk to site supervisors and project managers about specific needs.

When materials were returned to the warehouse at the end of the day, the warehouse team used a bin system to sort between tools in need of sharpening or cleaning and those that were ready to go back out into the field. A separate ladder management board listed every current job site and showed which ladders—all given proper names such as Elvis and Cary Grant—were where. Knowing what we had and where it was made us more disciplined. Instead of overbuying supplies for upcoming houses and then losing half of it in the warehouse, we were tracking materials and spending less.

A gutting kit box.

In 2012, while we were rebuilding homes in two states, it even felt like we had a little extra time to invest in ourselves. So, we got married. At the time, we were housesitting for friends in a lovely and large old historic home on Bayou St. John. We brought together old friends and new, blocked off the street, and got married. We even managed to have a honeymoon before getting back to work.

And just in time, we also realized that Brian was right. Our lead time on a house had been improving steadily over the months, just like he said it would if we redirected our attention. Lead time also dropped steeply after big improvement projects like the warehouse organization or after training on newly standardized work in the trades. And it improved steadily but slowly as we held our meetings every morning around the big production control board, talking about the Hendersons' house or the Davis'.

Our well-organized warehouse.

Superstorm Sandy

Then disaster struck again. Superstorm Sandy came barreling into New York and New Jersey at the end of 2012, killing 233 people. It became the second-costliest storm event in US history. We watched the devastation unfolding on the small television set in our hospital room, where Liz had just given birth to our son, Jack.

Zack said, "We really have to go help."

In the devastated neighborhoods of Far Rockaway Beach in New York, Zack and Reese May, a US Marine veteran and now our chief strategy and innovation officer, quickly found a group of neighbors who were already organized to help each other out. We

Workers after Superstorm Sandy.

partnered with this group, Friends of Rockaway, and shared our methods.[3] We helped create a warehouse and project tracking that were organized for the clients' benefit from the very beginning.

As our people from New Orleans rotated through positions in Missouri, New York, and New Jersey, we learned more from every location. New cadres of AmeriCorps members were trained in TPS techniques and brought new energy and ideas. Finally, our lead time dropped to 61 days—sometimes even a little less—and we started being able to tell people to pack their bags by a certain date when they would be going home. We were excited about our successes, but we knew we needed to find better ways to help communities recover faster.

Disaster recovery is an issue that is bound to affect everyone. In 2017, hurricanes were intensifying significantly faster than just 25 years earlier. Global wind speeds had increased by 5% since the mid-1990s, and extra water vapor in the atmosphere was making storms a lot wetter.[4] Our mission was more urgent than ever. Therefore, understanding and improving our processes were imperative. If there is one thing we have learned, it is that waiting and waste are the twin enemies of recovery.

3. Friends of Rockaway merged with SBP in 2016.
4. "Storms Are Getting Stronger," NASA Earth Observatory, accessed June 2017, https://earthobservatory.nasa.gov/Features/ClimateStorms/page2.php.

Let's Get You Home.
SBP's Integrated Model

The simplest way to understand the construction aspect of our work is to analogize it with the service or manufacturing industries. But instead of producing things or services, we create homecomings. As we have incorporated the respectful, problem-solving culture of TPS, we have discovered that our actions are substantially similar to for-profit companies: we identify customers, learn what they want, and try to deliver what they want with the least amount of wasted time and resources.

However, many of the pressures we face are different from those of an automotive manufacturer or a hospital. Businesses have a (mostly) predictable labor force. Our volunteer labor force might number 15 one week and 95 the next—and most of them are brand new to construction. And our client transactions are not so straight-forward as most order-fulfillment processes. So it will be useful to review a quick template of our integrated, nine-step model before we go further. This is not a perfect process, and we are always looking for improvements. But for now, it will be a good road map through our world.

Step 1. Find the client

When a hurricane or a tornado rips through a community, some houses will be left untouched while a next-door neighbor's is leveled. The impact on people is similar. In places like Far Rockaway or Joplin, we find that many people can recover on their own. Using a combination of private insurance and government disaster relief,

We create homecomings.

they find and hire contractors, help and get help from their neighbors, and come through the ordeal changed but still standing.

Our clients are in more precarious situations. They are usually elderly, disabled, or families with young children, stretched thin in time, money, and patience. They are uninsured or underinsured or have suffered contractor fraud. They own their home, need to stay there, and have enough income to keep up with basic utilities and maintenance but, like most Americans, do not have the cash reserves necessary for major repairs.

In the chaos immediately following a disaster, we find our clients, or our clients find us, largely through word of mouth. We met our first clients in 2006 through connections at the hippie tent.

SBP's Integrated Model

Step 1. Find the client

Step 2. Find the funding

Step 3. Finalize the scope of work and
all cost estimates

Step 4. Permitting

Step 5. Construction review

Step 6. Construction

Step 7. Client walk-through; punch list

Step 8. Final approval, funding

Step 9. Administrative closeout and
"welcome home"

Twelve years later, we were sending small teams into disaster areas as early as possible to assess needs and find the people in danger of falling through gaps in the safety net. We send representatives to community meetings and neighborhood resource fairs, and we create partnerships with other organizations such as Habitat for Humanity and government agencies.

We do a thorough application process on all potential clients, making sure they cannot afford to hire a contractor, have clear title on the property, and will be able to live independently once we are done. Some people need a little extra help from other organizations while in the rebuilding process. Our goal is to be flexible and adapt to the situation, while staying largely within our parameters.

Step 2. Find the funding

This involves matching funding from an ever-evolving list of public and private sources to a client family's own particular circumstances. Since 2010, much of the funding available from the federal government is *needs based* and comes with income caps. The money from *X fund* is only available to clients whose income equals *Y percent* of the area's median income. This is an area of frustration. We never know how long it will take to find funding, leaving everyone's plans locked in limbo.

When government funds are not available[5] or running low, we tap into private sources. Community foundations, United Way, the Red Cross, and local corporate partners often generously invest funds to support rebuilding for clients who otherwise have no path forward. If the client has large family or church networks, we help organize fundraising efforts through charity events or internet sites like GoFundMe.

When clients have compelling stories, we approach media outlets like newspapers or television shows. We have funded half of the cost of rebuilding a family home from donations generated after a single well-timed story in a newspaper or network news broadcast. Companies like Toyota, Farmers, Turner Construction, UPS, and Zurich Insurance have funded some of our most vulnerable clients. Some companies use volunteer weeks with us as team building exercises and can be moved to fund an entire project.

The critical point here is that we line up all the necessary funding *before* we begin construction. We used to dive headlong into projects with the idea that money would appear in time. But one time too

---

5. It generally takes at least 12 months until HUD funds are accessible for homeowners. HUD is working hard and creatively to expedite this process. Beginning in 2016, FEMA has innovated in important ways, freeing funds for repairs much earlier than previously available.

many we had to halt construction when money ran out. We found that stopping projects had so many negative consequences, both for the clients' emotional well-being and for our work, we make sure now that we have the money committed before we begin.

Step 3. Finalize the scope of work and all cost estimates

This is one of the more straightforward and controllable processes we have. It involves our director of construction walking the site, talking to the homeowner, and creating a final building plan and a scope of work. The scope of work states what we will do. If it is not in the scope, baring mistakes or unforeseen circumstances, we won't do the work.

At the end of this step, the homeowner knows exactly what we will and will not do. This is vital for managing clients' expectations. Then plans are drawn up and cost estimates completed.

Step 4. Permitting

Most of the grants we receive from government programs require that we complete environmental reviews on our work sites. This process begins by testing for lead and asbestos, locating the property on floodplain maps, and submitting our plans to local officials. This is another unknown time element for recovery. Particularly in the immediate aftermath of disaster, government agencies can be overwhelmed and permitting becomes disorganized.

We work diligently at creating partnerships with agencies but do not have the power to improve their processes. So, we aim for predictability. Being a frequent customer of New Orleans' "One Stop" department of permits and licensing, and having developed a good working rhythm there, we know we can depend on a one-week lead time for permitting.

Other agencies, in particular, ones that require environmental reviews in exchange for funding but are not necessarily experienced at reading building plans, might take 60–90 days or more. There are enough unknowns that can occur in this part of the process that it remains off-line from the schedule; only after all permits are signed off do we move a project onto the production board.

Step 5. Construction review

Once a project has a funder and has completed environmental reviews and building plans and we have an official Notice to Proceed—required for all projects, whether it is in-house or from an outside agency—we move to our production board and create the schedule that will guide us through the phases of building.

Every home has a time line posted on the production board, with job-by-job deadlines based on our best estimations. Now we know whether we are ahead or behind on every house, for each task, each day (see page 20). And perhaps more importantly, we can look at the board and see that three weeks from now, four houses will be ready for painting or drywall at the same time, so our volunteer coordinators need to make sure we have the necessary labor.

The production board is one area that we try to improve on a regular basis. However, using the board every morning has proved challenging for our front-line affiliates where disaster is more recent. It is an area for improvement.

For every project, we also create a site binder. This is a simple three-ring binder stored at the job site with all necessary information on the homeowners and their story, the complete scope of work, safety policies, construction standards, visual examples, and any special instructions. Our site supervisors are most often young people with little or no previous construction experience. Their job is to train and inspire groups of volunteers—ranging from retirees

On-site materials table with site binder.

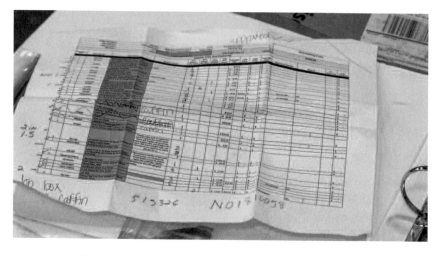

A detailed information sheet from a work site binder.

and teenagers to big men who are used to being in charge—to hang drywall, lay tile, or paint. We want our volunteers to be safe, work hard, and come away with a positive experience, knowing they have truly made a difference in the lives of the homeowners. So, we need to make sure that the site supervisors have all the information and support they need in order to get near-professional-level work from hardworking, often inexperienced volunteers.

Step 6. Construction

In order of how the work is accomplished:

A. Foundation. If work is required, we bring in professionals.

B. Framing. We bring in master carpenters in some communities but have also standardized the work and brought some of it in-house. With the help of AmeriCorps members, volunteers can follow standardized framing plans and build all the walls for a house in a day.

C. **Roof.** Professionals do this, mostly because the insurance costs of putting volunteers on a roof are prohibitive.

D. **Windows.** Installed by vendors or SBP, depending on the job.

E. **Rough-ins** for electrical, plumbing, HVAC. While we have standardized the plumbing and electrical work, we still use mostly outside professionals. This is a future opportunity for improvement, since bringing in outside people always inserts unpredictability to our schedules.

F. **Inspections.** These are required by the city, typically before we close up the walls.

G. **Wall finishing,** including insulation, drywall, mudding, and painting. With the right number of volunteers, this has become a remarkably predictable and satisfying part of the home process.

H. **Floors.** This involves a combination of tile, wood, and vinyl, usually done by AmeriCorps members and volunteers.

I. **Finish work** for plumbing and electrical includes installing faucets, sinks, toilets, electrical outlets, and light switches. This is mostly accomplished by tradespeople, either contractors or staff.

J. **Final inspections** and certificate of occupancy, issued by the city or county.

Note: Hiring is an ongoing challenge. We need contractors, electricians, and plumbers who fit our culture. Finding people who want to help others is easy. Finding ones open to change is much harder. Our journey has made it clear that we need people who are comfortable being uncomfortable. Being willing to innovate and to risk failure is more important than altruism.

Step 7. Client walk-through; punch list

Anyone who has purchased a brand-new house or has had extensive remodeling done knows about the punch list. This is the final to-do list, usually generated by the homeowner and production coordinator during the client walk-through. We might notice a door sticking, brush strokes in the paint, or a crooked light fixture. Our staff then schedules time to fix any and all issues.

The punch list moves incorrectly done tasks to the end of the project. This is an invitation to rework; rework is muda or waste. But the punch list is also a well-established tradition in the building industry. So, we track items on a rework board to identify patterns and facilitate the development of countermeasures.

Step 8. Final approval, funding

At one point near the end of construction, a representative of the funding agency walks through the home to ensure that we have done all of the things we said we would do in the scope of work and to ensure the work meets their quality standards. This is a necessary part of ensuring that everyone's expectations are met.

Step 9. Administrative closeout and "welcome home"

Finally, we make sure that utilities are on and properly working and that all necessary permits have the final signatures. Once the criteria of all stakeholders have been satisfied, we order the cake for the welcome home party, marking the end of recovery for our client and a return to normal life.

So there we are, start to finish. Our essential workflow has not changed a whole lot since we first conceived of putting all recovery services under one roof in 2006. What has evolved is our deeper understanding of our processes and the opportunities they contain for improvement. Encouraged by our partners at Toyota, and applying what we learned from TPS, we are building an organization of problem solvers at SBP, and that is what has changed everything.

Liz working with a group of volunteers.

Remodeling Our Culture
Becoming Client Driven

As should be evident, we have opportunities for improvement. Lots of them. In the past, tackling those opportunities always seemed too steep a climb. We were busy fixing houses; people were depending on us. Stopping to improve ourselves seemed a luxury.

Then our TSSC advisors turned our expectations upside down. It took time and effort and a level of discomfort to address problems the way Toyota did. But every problem solved gave us more time in a day. Even before lead time on a house went from 116 days to 61, we could feel things loosen up. We had more time in the week to think about other issues we wanted to attack, such as developing better volunteer engagement strategies or creating standardized organization in the work sites.

To keep that momentum going, we needed to become an organization of problem solvers. This was a far leap from having some nice guys from TSSC come in and tell us what to do. We couldn't just do TPS. We needed to adopt the ideas and values of TPS into our DNA. We needed to be problem solvers to our cores.

But we were not entirely comfortable with all of the language. For Liz, the term *continuous improvement* felt like a grind, like a hamster on an exercise wheel. So, we looked around at what other organizations did while following the TPS way. We learned that most ended up adopting their own language. Our friend and member of our board, Jerry Mattes, former president of UPS, talked about looking for problems to solve as *constructive dissatisfaction*.

Zack liked this term, except for the dissatisfaction part. Like the leaders at UPS, we wanted our people to be in consistent pursuit of something better. Zack thought about Frederick Douglass writing, "Where there is no struggle, there is no progress." He wanted to embrace the struggle—to encourage discontent—even while avoiding the sense that we were all rodents on wheels. So we arrived at *constructive discontent* to talk about problems and the search for improvement.

Constructive discontent became our ethos, woven into the fabric of our culture. We wanted it to become part of our identity. We had read in *Switch*, the business book about change by brothers Dan and Chip Heath, that the driver of decision making is not, as you would think, a rational choice assessment. Instead, what impels most decisions is identity. We ask ourselves, "What would a person like me do in a situation like this?"

To become an organization of problem solvers, talking about problems couldn't merely be something that we did. It had to be part of who we are; it had to be our identity. Being or living constructive discontent and adopting it as our identity would mean that problems were brought to the surface, not buried. We began wrapping up meetings with the question, "Is there any constructive discontent to talk about?"

Sure, this is just a nice way of asking whether there are any problems to discuss. But the positive language turned out to be really important. Our people had found it difficult to stick up a hand and say they had noticed a problem. Partly this was due to the fact that the majority of our team members are time-limited AmeriCorps members; some of them probably felt intimidated. But we also had a lot of optimistic, helpful people on staff who did not like to criticize others and could fall into a pattern of heroically taking on problems alone.

Embracing an identity of constructive discontent took talking about problems from being optional to being a core part of who we are and how we interact with the world. We needed a way to hardwire addressing problems into our culture. We needed people to want to uncover and talk about difficulties, to seek out problems—like hunting wild nutria. That's not a completely random analogy; there is a parallel here.

For those of you unacquainted with them, nutria are large semi-aquatic rodents that were once raised for their fur on an island off the coast of Louisiana. Then a hurricane smashed their fences and helped them spread to the mainland. Their status quickly changed from business asset to burrowing, destructive pests (aka river rats). They were everywhere, but people did not like to talk about them and nobody wanted their fur anymore. They were without value. The state, however, needed to address the issue of too many nutrias. So the state offered a bounty—cash money—for nutria tails. And the rodents became worthy of hunting.

The question is, how do we get people to hunt river rats—problems—without a bounty? The answer we found has two parts: 1) make problem hunting part of the training and deliverable work of our AmeriCorps members and staff and 2) adopt change on a personal level.

Let's start with the easy part, which is teaching problem hunting to our AmeriCorps members during their 10-month stint. This is a new idea for SBP and has only been implemented in New Orleans (as of this writing), but we are excited about the results so far.

We make a promise to AmeriCorps to give training in what we call "Life After AmeriCorps." It makes sense to teach TPS skills as part of this promise, even though it is a very large undertaking.[6]

---

6. We also teach résumé writing and job interview skills as part of this promise.

SBP has 50 full-time staff members (as of this writing) and more than 180 AmeriCorps members at any given time. That means we have 140% turnover every 10 months. To make it work, SBP staff had to learn how to be TPS coaches to mentor AmeriCorps members through problem-hunting training projects.

We had a finite amount of time with every AmeriCorps member, so we knew we needed to be very clear about our expectations from the beginning and plan for each step of their education. For instance, site supervisors received six weeks of training before they worked on their own. This included specific instruction on construction processes, how to teach and inspire volunteers to build houses, and what we mean by TPS.

During AmeriCorps orientation in New Orleans (which happens four to six times a year to accommodate staggered starting dates) we have a TSSC advisor come in and give a half day of training on the philosophy of TPS. Members learn respect for people, bringing problems to the surface, and knowing whether we are ahead or behind. They learn about identifying waste and how to solve problems. Even if they do not have perfect recall following this training, they have at least been introduced to the ideas. (The TSSC advisor's other day is spent coaching our staff mentors.)

AmeriCorps members usually need between one to three months to master their jobs as site supervisors, supply and logistics coordinators, or in client services. After that—right around their fourth or fifth month with us—it is time for a member to identify at least one problem to solve. That's when we start mentoring them through problem solving, forming teams, and completing each step of the process of implementing countermeasures.

The first step is identifying a problem, using observation and collected data, and then writing a description of it that is specific yet open-ended. We do not want anyone to presume a solution or cast blame in their problem statement, so members receive coaching as they write.

Then we put together a team to address the problem. Sometimes these teams have members from across the functional areas, other times everyone is in the same department. Team makeup is decided by the nature of the problem and whether a coach thinks the team needs an outside perspective. Time, or lack thereof, and availability are also factors.

Teams are taught to work through each of the following seven problem-solving steps together:

1. Go see the problem at the point of occurrence.
2. Collect facts (a record of events) and data (measurements of those events) regarding the problem.
3. Set a future target condition and date for completion.
4. Perform root cause analysis using the *5 Whys*.
5. Analyze the factors involved, including the people, the materials or machines, and the methods used.[7]
6. Analyze the proposed countermeasures for effects on the organization.
7. Create a plan: who does what, when, in order to put the countermeasures in place?

It is important to note that Toyota emphasizes finding countermeasures to problems, not solutions. A solution sounds like there is one right answer. But we know that a better countermeasure to a problem might be found in the future and that any countermeasure is likely to create new problems, even as it "solves" the immediate one.

---

7. We refer to this as "man, machine, and method" to make it easier to remember.

For instance, one problem we worked on in 2016 involved capturing information from volunteers. From every volunteer at a work site, we wanted a signed waiver and five points of data: name, email, phone number, home address, and age range. Our record of getting this information was consistently inconsistent, but we did not really understand why. A team tackled the issue by examining the most common point of defect: the paper waivers volunteers filled out on their day of work. People who signed up online could not submit their forms without filling in each item. Paper waivers did not have the same safeguard.

Here is what the team found:

Problem

Inconsistent volunteer information gathering with paper waivers filled out on the day of work.

Collected Facts

On 100 paper waivers selected at random, information was illegible or missing much of the time. Specific numbers:

Name: 89/100
Email: 61/100
Phone: 61/100
Address: 52/100
Age range: 81/100

Target

100% of registrations should have all 5 data points within 35 days of the team's report.

Root Cause Analysis

1. We are not receiving all five data points from volunteers who register on paper. *Why?*
2. We are not getting complete, legible data. *Why?*
3. We can't force volunteers to give complete, legible data. *Why?*
4. We use paper registrations that offer the option to not give full data. *Why?*
5. Online registration takes too long to use at on-site orientation.

Process Analysis

Man: Do volunteers fill it out accurately?

   No. Blank or not legible.

Machine: Is the registration form an effective tool?

   No. Too long and repetitive.

Method: Is the technique effective?

   No. This was the team's chosen focus.

Proposed Countermeasures

1. Make "day of" form
2. Make link for phone sign-ups
3. Make new paper version
4. Beta test internal/external

Countermeasures Deliverable

What	Who	When	Status
Make "day of" form	Judy	12/5	
Make link for phone sign-ups	MVL	12/6	
Make new paper version	KA	12/6	
Beta test internal/external	KA/MVL	12/7, 12/12	
Review data after trial	VC team	12/13	

This was just one problem-finding/countermeasure project out of more than 60 typically done in a year. Teams have tackled issues like inadequate training for construction coordinators, the lack of affordable housing for AmeriCorps members in new disaster areas, and how to find electrical outlets after they have been covered over by drywall.

Training these intelligent and passionate young people in TPS thinking and then setting them loose to find countermeasures for our problems is a powerful force, which can lead to unexpected solutions. But sometimes, if a person is used to being in charge, this can cause heartburn.

The second answer to the question "How do we get people to hunt river rats without a bounty?" involves adopting change on a personal level. Painful, deeply personal change, as Zack discovered. And since this is Zack's story, Liz will slip out of the frame and let him tell it.

Zack

As a criminal defense lawyer, my job was to win. My clients were indigent, and many had been subjected to one injustice after another. In the courtroom and in negotiations with prosecutors, I could prevent or reduce imprisonment, or I could fail. That was my world view before Liz and I started SBP. You win or you lose. I operated in a zero-sum game.

All of us carry the past with us; my training as a litigator came with me. My success or failure had a serious impact on people's lives. Results mattered more than how you got there, as long it was legal. I was accustomed to arguing.

The first time I recognized this as an impediment as a leader at SBP was in 2011, when Sylvester came to work with us. He did not give directives or ultimatums; he would ask questions. He might say, "Zack, explain to me how communicating in that way will help solve the problem."

I would try to listen, but there was one issue in particular that really got to me. Volunteers often come to us in floods. During school holidays or in the weeks after a new disaster, we could get deluged with service groups wanting to pitch in. They were willing to travel, to put their safety in our hands. In exchange, those groups wanted—and deserved—a meaningful experience. It was our job to give that to them, to make sure they knew their efforts were useful and appreciated.

I never wanted to say no to volunteers. In fact, I believed that saying "We don't need you" was a terrible lie. They were needed, desperately. We could not send people away thinking that the recovery was complete. And so I dug in on this point: never say no to volunteers.

Liz would point out that we were too often chasing our tails. If we had 300 volunteers signed up for a week and only 10 houses under construction, we would start new projects, even if that meant stopping work again two weeks later. It was chaos. Liz wasn't wrong. But I had a dozen arguments at the ready for why we could not tell volunteers that we did not need them.

Zack leading a training session.

Sylvester and Liz wanted a team to tackle the issue. I was afraid the team would choose to send volunteers away. That would be a grave injustice. Even talking about it frightened me. Sylvester tried to help by asking me questions like, "Do you trust the team? What are the team members motivated by? Does the team know what success looks like?"

Liz spoke to me in firmer tones, saying something like, "Either do it all yourself or get out of the team's way."

I held my breath and let the team proceed. I can still remember sitting in the team's final presentation as a dozen arguments and emotions bounced around in my head. But their proposed solution was simple: *double shifts*. To accommodate big labor influxes, staff and AmeriCorps members would work two shifts of six hours each, allowing every volunteer to do solid work without over-taxing our people. The solution was simple, elegant, and a revelation. We implemented the plan, and, with few modifications, it was still working seven years later.

This did not change me overnight, however. I still had a tendency to litigate issues. Arguing was my natural response to being presented with problems. We got to a place where staff members told me one thing and Liz another.

Liz was not happy. I was still sure that my arguments were rock-solid. If I had not been in love with my business partner, I do not think I would have been able to hear that I was charging down the wrong path.

It was late 2011 when the chair of our board, Kirk Menard, told me that I would be undergoing a 360 review. It was a great opportunity he said. I felt a little sick to my stomach, but there was no backing out.

Board members, senior staff, Liz, team members from various levels in the organization—it seemed like half the organization— were invited to discuss my management style. I learned from them that I had boundless energy and I used that energy to sometimes run right over people. I was focused (on my own concerns). I cared deeply for our clients (not so much for anyone else). I was a terrible listener with a tendency to cross-examine. In short, I was like a television version of a boss.

I was hurt and a little scared that I had gone too far to recover anyone's good graces. But Kirk told me, "The worse your review, the more it indicates that your team trusts you and has hope for you. If they all say you're fine, they have no hope."

I believed him and resolved to try a new style. Fortunately, 360 reviews require an individual development plan with a clear path to follow. One of my development objectives was "Be consistent when receiving news and providing feedback." I had five activities to help me achieve this objective:

1. Articulate what "being consistent" looks like.
2. Commit publicly to the team to work on consistency.
3. Pause between receipt of information and response.
4. Make sure that I eat before meetings. (Nobody likes a "hangry" boss.)
5. Remember that team members are just as committed as I am and that there are different and valid ways to show commitment.

For me, the 360 review process was very much like how we address problems (identify a problem, collect data from the source, analyze the data, create countermeasures, and set a schedule to put them in place). Discovering that others were willing to help me overcome my shortcoming took some of the sting out of the fact that I was the identified problem.

In fact, I took to the idea of being personally accountable to everyone around me with the zeal of the newly converted. I was constantly asking people for feedback. At the end of an interaction about construction schedules or some new initiative, I would ask, "Do you feel like I was really listening? Did you get an opportunity to tell me what you think or whether there were problems?"

I may have gone a little overboard. However, Liz thinks I did such a thorough job of modeling the behavior we want—respectful, problem seeking—that I helped accelerate the culture change at SBP. I hope that is the case, because we have discovered that creating a positive, problem-seeking culture encourages flexibility and creativity. And these are important attributes in an organization that relies on direct labor from a source that is often as unpredictable as they are enthusiastic: volunteers.

Putting up a ceiling takes teamwork.

A Trickier Problem
Volunteers at the Front Line

Teams of AmeriCorps members cannot address every problem we encounter. Some of our thorniest issues are rooted in the very structure of our work and require more focused attention. Using volunteers as our biggest source of touch labor is a great example.[8]

SBP derives many benefits from using volunteers. We are introduced to people from all over the country who want to help. They raise funds for our clients, tell their communities about our work, and spread the word that disaster recovery is on-going. And all of this happens before they show up to build walls and paint them. We have had groups come back every year for a decade. These relationships are crucial to our work.

The downside is that we have little control over how many volunteer workers we have and what their skills might be. This would be more manageable if we had a consistent flow of knowable tasks. If we just needed people to paint a consistent number of walls that were always prepped and ready for work, for instance, we could adjust our project time lines around our workforce numbers.

The trouble is that we always have a variety of projects moving through various stages. One project might be rebuilding an entire house; the next job might be installing a new roof and painting the exterior. The new house project will not need volunteers until week four, and then it will need 12 volunteers a day for six weeks.

8. By "touch labor" we mean the people who are laying hands on material and transforming it.

The exterior paint job might need volunteers in week two (after the roof is done) and can handle eight volunteers a day for three weeks. But we cannot predict with any confidence exactly when a job might start because we must wait for an official Notice to Proceed, usually granted by an outside agency.

For instance, let's look at our rebuilding operations in New Orleans. Our most common sources of funding in New Orleans are grants that are managed and issued by the city. So, most of our projects move through these stages of pre-construction:

1. SBP client assessments
2. SBP funding reviews
3. City of New Orleans client assessment
4. City environmental review (test for lead paint and assess flood insurance needs)
5. City construction review to approve SBP project scope
6. Notice to Proceed issued

We cannot begin work until this Notice to Proceed is issued, and then we must start within seven days. Sometimes we can wait a few days longer to begin construction. But in general, when the city issues that Notice to Proceed, we are expected to start work within the week. Lining up labor is our responsibility.

By now, we know our volunteer labor force is robust in the spring and early summer. We set target capacity at 100 volunteers per shift in New Orleans with, ideally, a limit of 12 volunteers for every AmeriCorps supervisor on site. From Mardi Gras through July, we usually reach or exceed our limit of volunteers. From mid-August through the winter holidays, we average less than half of that labor force.

For years, we have been trying to find a way to plan ahead, to shape the schedule so that we have the right mix of volunteer-friendly jobs. We also know from working with Toyota that our goal is one-piece flow. For us that means starting a new job just as we finish a job: one in, one out. But the mix of job types, labor availability, and the cadence of those Notices to Proceed made one-piece flow seem elusive.

Then in 2017, Liz had a workflow revelation. It started out badly. The City of New Orleans had a specific grant that was paying for about 10 SBP projects that were working through the stages of pre-construction. It seemed to be going at the expected pace when we got a notice saying that, in addition to individual project environmental reviews, the entire grant project required another environmental review. The cohort of projects would be held up for months and then released in bulk. That meant we would get all the Notices to Proceed at once. Liz held up her hands and asked the city to wait.

It was like time stopped. Instead of jumping on each project—no matter what it was—as it came out of the city gates, we had a pool of projects. We could pick and choose. We asked for Notices to Proceed on a few projects at a time, creating a mix that worked with our planned labor levels. This was exactly the type of system Liz had been aiming to achieve.

The problem was, we could not create a permanent pool of waiting projects. The city does not like to let projects sit around after decisions have been made. Conditions that guided the original decision could change; money could become scarce. And we could not in good conscience make clients wait for our convenience.

We thought we needed to control the rate at which jobs came on line in order to make the best use of our highly variable labor. And that seemed implausible, at best. Then we discovered that we were not seeing the whole picture. Liz was invited to a conference for leaders at TSSC and attended a workshop about leveling demand. She learned how Toyota keeps a steady rate of production with a standardized scheduling practice called *heijunka*.

For instance, in Toyota's Mississippi plant where Corollas are made, workers produce, on average, more than 520 cars per day. That's roughly one car every 55 seconds coming off the production lines. This matches the rate of demand for new Corollas. If volume increases or decreases, the plant runs more or fewer minutes while the standardized work and the work cadence remain the same. This kind of heijunka is known as "leveling by volume."

To keep the pace steady, cars in progress move through the factory at a set speed, and workers add parts to the cars as they move through the work stations. Within the Corolla model, there were many variations, e.g., leather or fabric seats, automatic or manual transmission, air conditioning, sunroofs, etc. These options called for variations in work content. Assembly workers might need extra time to create and install a wiring harness for a 12-speaker luxury sound system, while the cars move past at that steady timed rate. If every fifth car requires the harness, the workers can keep pace. If three cars in a row need the harness, the work cannot be completed without stopping the assembly line.

Factory leaders create a balanced line with a mix of models that takes into account the constraints of labor. This type of heijunka is called "leveling by mix." It is a way to think about presenting work so it can proceed smoothly, without anyone rushing to finish or standing around waiting.

Back in New Orleans, Liz pulled together a cross-functional group of senior leaders to talk through what she had learned. Essentially, she taught us the heijunka concept and then asked for help applying it to home rebuilding.

SBP does not have anything like Toyota's factories and volumes of production. But if we look at what we do make—homecomings—we saw that we could divide the jobs into model types. Some homecomings involve major work and we touch the entire house. Others might need only replacing a poorly constructed roof or repairing a bad plumbing job in the second bathroom.

Now that we could confidently predict how much time various jobs would take, we could divide our work into four models:

- Minor: involving fewer than 30 days work
- Moderate: 30–60 days work
- Major: 60–90 days work
- New construction: 90+ days

To try to create a steady cadence, we set a target to begin six new jobs every month with a mix of models. In April 2017, we started seven new jobs, all minor; in May, we started four new minor jobs, one major rebuild, and one new construction.

As you can see (on page 64), we forecast ahead as to when each job would end on a project tracking board. Every job on the bottom row has a corresponding slot on the top row. This is our prompt to have another job ready to go—one in, one out. We also have a kind of parking lot of jobs that are in the city's pre-construction approval process, to make sure we keep an eye on what is coming up soon. Keeping this workflow cadence up to date means talking every week about what is coming through the city's pipeline, our mix of jobs and labor, and when projects will end—signaling the need for another job to fill its spot.

Mix-model project tracking board

As we go forward, we will learn more about how this leveling-by-mix approach can get us closer to one-piece flow. If it works the way we hope, we will develop a more reliable working cadence and therefore more capacity for creating innovative new building ideas and programs. This will help us meet our central mission of shrinking the time between disaster and recovery for families like the Lees in the Algiers neighborhood of New Orleans.

Mr. Lee's Front Porch
New Standardization in Building

There was much history to be seen from 95-year-old Edward Lee Sr.'s front porch, if you knew where to look. Just across the street was once the plantation where Mr. Lee's father was born into slavery during the Civil War. Down the road had stood the old Stanton Plantation, where Mr. Lee was born while his dad, already in his 60s, worked the sugar cane and corn fields for $8 a week. Those fields became houses long ago.

Look to the left and down the block and you can almost see Pastor Morris Gastinell's old house. He had a lovely daughter named Lucille. Mr. Lee wooed her and they were married in 1941.

Then Mr. Lee went off to war. He served for four years, nine months, and 27 days—he was certain of those numbers—on navy patrol craft, both in the Mediterranean and Pacific Oceans. His unit fished live mines out of harbors, mostly, and he had the shrapnel scars to show for it. After the war, he was glad to come home to the Algiers neighborhood of New Orleans and get back to making a life with Lucille.

With help from the G.I. Bill, Mr. Lee attended the Booker T. Washington Trade School, where he learned carpentry and masonry. He built his house on Sullen Place with help from his father-in-law. He built another house two doors down for his mother. Later, as a contractor, he built dozens more on both sides of the Mississippi River. The Lees had seven children while living in this house, four girls and three boys, and sent all of them to college.

Mr. Lee's original, storm-damaged house

Well, not *this* house, exactly. The house that Mr. Lee built—carefully braced and strutted against disaster—was damaged pretty badly in Hurricane Katrina. A lovely old tree just off the back steps went through a back window, and the roof was ripped off. There was an infestation of red ants, and the house took on water. Mr. Lee and his daughter Veronica rode out the storm in Houston. They returned to Sullen Place two months later to begin cleaning up.

In his mid-80s when Katrina hit, Mr. Lee had a list of what he could fix and where he needed help; he thought he would be all right. But like so many others, he found that the money offered by Road Home federal grants was not enough to make all the repairs. Materials were expensive and hard to find. He got started but lost everything to contractors who demanded cash up-front and didn't do the work. That knocked him back. His daughter Veronica had moved in and had become his caretaker when we met them in 2015.

Ten years after Hurricane Katrina, Mr. Lee's house was half gutted, and sheets took the place of glass in some windows. A toilet drained under one of the bedrooms. Mold and termites had seriously undermined the subfloors and joists. Mr. Lee had been living in what should have been a condemned building for a decade. This was no way to treat a veteran.

Alarmed by the growing rate of homelessness among veterans across the United States, we launched a *Sixteen for '16* campaign to build or rebuild homes for 16 veterans in Louisiana, South Carolina, Texas, New Jersey, and New York within the year 2016. Mr. Lee became our emotional touchstone for the campaign, and his house became a kind of trial run for another new idea.

For a number of years, we had been distressed by the pace and cost of certain practices in the home-building industry. Framing walls, for instance, always seemed to take longer and cost more than was necessary. For a standard three bedroom, two bathroom, 1,300-square-foot stick-built house, it might take three weeks and cost about $18,000 for rough framing of a home, and produce piles of scrap lumber. Each time, it was like reinventing walls—within code, of course—from scratch. We would watch teams of professional framers through our newly TPS-sensitized vision and think there had to be a better way.

In the spring of 2015, at a Lean Enterprise Institute conference in New Orleans, we met leaders from Turner Construction—an international building firm that completes huge projects such as the new Whitney Museum of American Art and the Madison Square Garden transformation—and took our first steps toward that better way. We did not yet know Mr. Lee. In fact, the problem we were trying to solve when we began collaborating with Turner was Zack's favorite issue: what to do with uneven resources.

When we had a lot of volunteers at once but not enough for a double shift, or when weather caused havoc on a work site, ensuring that everyone had meaningful work was an issue. During the rainy season in New Orleans, we started looking at our warm, dry warehouse as a resource. It was a good place to work.

Fortunately, we were developing this corporate partnership with Turner Construction. During a series of conference calls to explore how we could work together, the idea of pre-fabricated walls came up. With the expertise of people like Kurt Gavalier, the national lean manager for Turner, we created a template and standardized work for building a wall.

"We figured out the best spacing for studs, did some color coding, and created a list of cuts to do on a saw," Kurt says. "Then Sean Dugas (director of design and construction) and I built it. The next day, we had volunteers build it. Then we refined the process. We wanted to make it so that anyone could walk up to a pile of wood and make a good wall. When we took three AmeriCorps members who had no power-tool experience and they built a wall, cut-to-finish in about an hour, we knew the plan would work."

With additional improvements to the process, our team created a system in which volunteers could reliably build a solid wall panel in about four minutes. Walls with a window could be built in five minutes. We expanded on the experiment and found we could build all the walls for a house in half a day, raise the walls on a home site in another day, and put roof trusses on it—all for under $90,000 for total construction of a house. And in the end we have one five-gallon bucket's worth of waste. (This last point has become particularly important as Liz has been pushing us toward a zero-landfill approach to building.)

Mr. Lee's new house, completed in 76 days.

Soon we were standing on Mr. Lee's front lawn and breaking the bad and good news to him. The bad news was that the walls he had hammered into place in 1946 were no longer viable. The house needed to be razed. The good news was that, with the help of our prefab approach to framing and our *Sixteen for '16* fund-raising, we could put a new house in its place in just a few months.

SBP finished Mr. Lee's house in 76 days. Because of the work we had been doing with Toyota, learning to find problems and follow through with countermeasures, learning to see opportunities for standardization and be disciplined about it, and working with other organizations in the lean community like Turner, we were as good as our word.

Celebrating Mr. Lee's homecoming

In May 2016, Mr. Lee and his daughter Veronica came home to a brand-new house, safe and sound. Until his passing in early 2018, from that front porch Mr. Lee greeted neighbors he had known for decades and looked out over the land where his family had lived and worked for more than 150 years.

The people at SBP had to be willing to take big risks, to make profound changes to our organization and work processes, to make this happen. We found that change is powerful, but a little scary too. With big change can come instability, and there are many aspects of our organization that we want to keep. This led us to another challenge: how to keep innovating rapidly without sacrificing stability and identity? As we worked to confront this problem, we once again had help from an unlikely source.

The Sum of Our Parts
Standard Training for a Unified Culture

Embracing constructive discontent requires that an organization accept a state of constant change. On this, SBP has doubled down. From the beginning, we adopted a business model that utilized two forms of temporary labor: volunteers and the AmeriCorps members who supervise their work. This model has assets and liabilities.

Our heavy lifters are enthusiastic and inexpensive, but they are constantly leaving. Volunteers might stay for a week. AmeriCorps members generally make a 10-month commitment. During their time with us, everyone is encouraged to improve our processes. As new people enter SBP, they change elements of our work and then leave us again, necessarily different.

An organization that undergoes this constant transformation is like a river coming down a mountain. The water, the fish, the leaves floating in the current are new every time you blink your eyes. Reeds grow and die. The river's course shifts a little or a lot with every rainy season. But the river's essential nature does not change.

With this in mind, the question for us has been, how do we retain our identity, our best ideas, and the positive aspects of our culture within a constant state of flux—while at the same time, how can we prevent being static as we build and improve processes for everything?

This is where TPS standardization tools have served us well, particularly when it comes to training. Early on in SBP's existence, we recognized that this was the kind of work that attracts intensely passionate people. But many of these people are restless. When they move on to the next thing they want to explore, they often take all their accumulated knowledge with them. Lots of organizations have this problem of institutional experience walking out the door, but our situation seemed extreme.

When we started working with AmeriCorps in 2009, our turnover further intensified. In 2010, when we were granted 78 AmeriCorps members, our standard training for new members was a two-day general orientation led by Sarah Sievert, AmeriCorps program manager. All members served 10-month terms but arrived in cohorts staggered throughout the year, and so we had about four of these orientations a year.

"It was just me talking at them, back then," Sarah remembers. "I would introduce the client services work, go through a sample application, then lead them through building a house. Members referred to me as their manager. It was just me talking and too much information all at once."

After orientation, she would hand out the SBP manual we created and assign all the new members to shadow a person doing their job.[9] Learning as you work is not a bad model. But our reliance on one-on-one training meant that a new member learned what one person knew and how that one person had interpreted the job and the mission. Results were uneven. AmeriCorps members usually started their tenure with fire and purpose. But after a few months, important parts of the training and work processes could be forgotten. If they lost the sense of why they did this work, it was harder to keep them with us.

---

9. Find downloadable copies of our resources at: sbpusa.org/what-we-do/prepare.

Then the tornado touched down in Joplin, Missouri, and we were suddenly onboarding AmeriCorps members 700 miles away. Sarah could not be in two places at once for orientation. So we evolved. She brought managers from client services, construction, and logistics in to talk to the new classes for part of the training and relied on the local director to run the show. It was better, but still it was not enough. The training wasn't interactive. We did not help managers prepare their presentations or ask for feedback.

We would try new methods for one class and feel like it was successful and add another teaching technique to the next class and think that went pretty well, too. Different people would be called on to teach, and they all emphasized different aspects of the work.

Sarah Sievert running an orientation meeting.

In the end, we relied too much on the idea that people would read their manuals and job descriptions for direction. Our process lacked control. From talking to AmeriCorps members, we knew that they had different ideas of what our organization was really trying to achieve. Everyone knew we rebuilt houses for people after natural disasters. But why we do that and how (through problem solving and standardized, visible work processes) was important to know, too.

Sometimes we lost AmeriCorps members before their 10-month term was completed. The job requires a great deal of energy, and the financial compensation is low enough that most members qualify for and receive federal food assistance. If they lost sight of why they were doing this work, it was easy to lose heart and find a way out.

In 2011, when we were granted 72 members in Louisiana, we had a 79.2% retention rate. That means 57 people successfully completed their terms of service. In September 2012, as we were expanding into new disaster areas, we jumped to getting 132 AmeriCorps members.[10] That year, as we started work in New York and New Jersey, our retention rate dropped to 72.7%.

Sarah did all of the orientations she could but relied more on new on-site managers to train new members. Managers often asked Sarah what the groups wanted to hear, and she realized there were many different ways to answer this question. With help from our Toyota advisors, we understood that this was an opportunity to rethink and improve our training.

Taking the original lessons we learned about standardization in our morning meetings around the big production board, we applied the concepts to how we train new people. We needed to perform training the same way every time so that we could make targeted

10. In 2017, our annual grant was up to 180 AmeriCorps members a year.

changes based on what was working or not. And we needed to treat each new class as we would a morning meeting at the production board, asking what we could do to make this group successful.

Sarah began stabilizing the process by pulling together a working group to rewrite the manuals with a greater emphasis on how each job was accomplished in detail. In each department, such as volunteer services, construction, and client services, Sarah or one of the team members talked to a supervisor about how the work was done, observed members who did it well, and captured all the particulars they could. For volunteer coordinators, for instance, they broke down the different phone calls that AmeriCorps members made to incoming volunteer groups. There were confirmation calls to help groups plan their visits and outreach calls to seek fresh help from groups we have worked with before. We needed each call to convey specific messages, and now the manual laid that out.

Manuals for site supervisors detailed the daily work of inspiring volunteer groups, keeping everyone safe, and teaching construction techniques. Best practices for morning icebreakers with volunteers were captured, as well as on-site materials organization. Manuals for members in client services explained the client application and approval process. They showed how to gather a client's information and create a presentation to help the entire client services team decide if they should move forward with a project. The manuals got better, but we still needed to present the big picture.

We realized that part of our attrition problem stemmed from personalities. Some people we brought in were not comfortable with change, confrontation, and talking about problems. We started asking applicants more directed questions, seeking those who were comfortable being uncomfortable.

Then Zack temporarily took on the task of training AmeriCorps members about why we work the way we do. For orientation meetings in New Orleans, he developed a talk that focused first on the new members, on why they chose to come to SBP, and how their work would make a real difference in people's lives. He began orientation by acknowledging that the job the AmeriCorps members signed up for is hard. They chose it, in fact, because it is hard.

By 2016, there were nine applicants for every one person SBP engaged, and we looked for people who wanted to be challenged, who were not satisfied with the status quo. These people would fit SBP's mission because they understood and embraced the constructive discontent that leads to unearthing and solving problems.

Zack told the new classes, "We have learned through TPS that the best ideas come from the shop floor, and you are the shop floor; you are the front lines."

Going around the room, he asked each person to tell the story of the hardest thing they ever did, of obstacles, failures, and successes. In these sessions, we heard stories of growing up in drug-addicted households and breaking free of abusive relationships to join AmeriCorps. One young man from an Ivy League university told us of growing up with a single mother who sacrificed every day so that he could have a successful career. Telling his mother that he wanted to live a life of service to others instead of joining a Wall Street firm was terrifying; he was not sure he could face her disappointment. He did, however, and eventually found the acceptance he hoped for.

Knowing that they had each faced daunting personal challenges made it easier for them to see themselves as people who embrace struggle, as people who are unafraid to face problems. In fact, Zack told them, it was already part of their identity; they just had not articulated it yet.

Zack then talked about SBP's core values:

1. We believe all problems are solvable.
2. We do work the way we would want it done for our grandparents or loved ones.
3. We share what we learn, both inside and outside of the organization.

During those two days of orientation, a senior staff member introduced the concepts of TPS, translated some of the Japanese terms, and showed them how we find and address problems. Kyle Carson, our manager of AmeriCorps and HR in Louisiana, did the training. Kyle was responsible for interviewing and hiring every member of the class, so we knew he had their attention as he taught them how to identify waste and how we address problems, including asking the 5 Whys.

Members then moved on to their departments for specialized training. Site supervisors, as part of the construction department, began right away by building a table from scrap wood. This is the first thing we do on every job site, and it gives everyone an opportunity to become familiar with tools and basic building skills. Once the table is built, we use blue tape to mark out sections for different tools and label them: measuring tapes, pencils, utility knives. Caulk guns and caulk, mudding supplies, and painting materials are grouped under the table. Screwdrivers and wrenches are separated and stored in construction buckets.

If possible, we have the class open a brand-new home site so that they can experience the first big delivery of materials from the warehouse. They learn the need for organization pretty quick.

Organized on-site tools.

Project managers (staff who supervise several site supervisors) instruct members in the use of two on-site whiteboards that are now standard at every work site. One board is separated into sections: goals for the day, goals for the week, materials needed, and questions for the project manager. Since the project manager usually splits her time between four and six sites, having questions waiting on the board has been a big time saver. The second board is devoted to safety, which the site supervisor uses every morning to enhance the two-minute safety talk with volunteer groups—another best practice that has become standardized work.

Example of an on-site welcome whiteboard.

In the volunteer department, members focus on learning how to make contact with incoming volunteer groups. These point-of-contact calls are critical to ensuring that we have reliable front-line labor to finish houses. We want volunteers to know that they are valued, that they are changing the lives of our client families, and that they can help us with fundraising. It is the job of volunteer coordinators to convey all of this.

National volunteer department manager Judy Martens trained new members by explaining each type of volunteer group phone call—from first contact to visit confirmation and final planning—and going over the important messages to impart point by point. Her volunteer coordinators began their tenure with all the information they needed. But there were many calls to make and many elements to each call. Inevitably, important pieces of information were forgotten as weeks went by.

Before SBP, Judy was an attorney. Before that, she was a boat captain sailing vessels around the Atlantic and Caribbean. She is very thorough and organized. While thinking about how to ensure that her coordinators remembered all the pertinent information of their different phone calls, she realized that it was all right there in the manual. Coordinators just needed what sailors use: repetition and cross-checking.

Judy took elements of each phone call, broke them down into a list, and started training off the list. Then she put herself into the system as the leader of a faux volunteer group. As coordinators cycled through their list of calls to make, sometimes Judy's name came up. Coordinators recognized Judy's name, of course, and knew the next call would be a checkup on their standard work. They would call her and work the script. Judy would then score them on every element and use it both to coach the coordinator and to inform her own training techniques.

Every coordinator makes a confirmation call about a month before a volunteer group is scheduled to arrive. This call begins by thanking the group leader for their willingness to help, asking about their inspiration to build houses with SBP, and expressing our ongoing need. When time allows, the coordinator offers details about various homes that we are working on. The goal is to get to know the personality of the group and to let them know about our clients and us.

The coordinator then asks about the group's travel plans, housing, logistics, the number of volunteers coming, and their ages. This is to help us set them up with an appropriate project. For instance, we have discovered that a group of high school students is perfectly capable of drywalling a kitchen and dining room, but we would not ask the same of a group with people who cannot lift heavy things over their heads. The coordinator confirms dates and then talks about how the group might leverage their impact for the upcoming trip by hosting a fundraising event. They might talk about what other groups have done or offer to send information packets.

These calls require both upbeat energy and attention to detail. Judy has found that by checking in regularly, she can confirm that elements of the call are not forgotten. She can also coach coordinators whose energy might be waning or who might be losing sight of the reason we do this work.

In TPS, Judy's method of regular observation of standardized work is referred to as *kamishibai*, which can be translated from the Japanese as "paper theater" and refers to visual aids used by storytellers. Kamishibai boards are visual prompts telling team leaders to observe standardized work and record whether it is being followed faithfully.

Judy does not have a board for visual cues; instead, she puts her name into the system to be called on a regular basis. The calls she receives from her coordinators are her cue to observe. She says, "I learned that regular checkins are really important. People might know what they have to do, but if they are not observed, some really important parts of the process will drop away."

Other departments arrived at similar methods, but the route was varied. In construction, for instance, some AmeriCorps members become construction coordinators, there to assist in getting permits from the city, synchronizing activity for home sites between various departments, and coordinating schedules with outside tradespeople. It requires a healthy dose of self-direction, and some people can get a bit lost in the job.

Then one day in the summer of 2016, a young AmeriCorps member named Chelsea Loa knocked on Liz's door and asked whether she could have a word. Liz offered her a seat and did very little prompting before Chelsea said simply, "I've been here for two months, and I'm still not sure what my job is."

Chelsea understood the basic parameters of her role but did not understand how she was adding value. She desperately wanted to be of service but instead felt that she ran around not quite getting things accomplished. She had to go back to the city's water utility office four times, for instance, before they actually had everything they needed in order to turn on the water in one of the client houses.

At the end of Chelsea's story, it was clear to Liz that there had been gaps in Chelsea's training and that most of her unhappiness had to do with her inability to produce tangible results. In her prior job as a barista, she had been trained in a very methodical fashion, with checklists and new information given at regular intervals. She was happy in her old job. Sure, it was just making coffee, but she knew what she was doing and how she added value.

So, Liz gave Chelsea authority to develop new training that would address problems, using her barista experience as a template. Chelsea went back to the manual and created a training program with a series of steps, goals, core messages, and lessons. As a novice construction coordinator learned a new aspect of the job, it would be accompanied by a checklist that could be used both as a quiz to gauge understanding and as a standardized reminder. This way, the construction coordinator could check that they had every bit of necessary documentation before heading to the water utility offices.

Chelsea beta-tested her checklist method on the next incoming construction coordinator. She learned even more in the process of teaching her new colleague and then enlisted his help to make changes in the training. Together, they plan to test their system again on the next new member. (We successfully engaged Chelsea for a second AmeriCorps term.)

Another opportunity to standardize training came when one of our talented site supervisors broke her foot while on vacation. Casey Leppo, a former figure skating coach from Maryland with a lot of energy, was suddenly anchored to her desk. She was on her second 10-month AmeriCorps rotation, and she knew from listening to complaints during weekly site-supervisor meetings about the need for standardization. She thought she could help with this and was encouraged to take it on.

"We only have six weeks of training and can't cover everything that can possibly happen on a job site. Once, I had to install a toilet and had no idea how to do that and had to Google it," Casey remembers. "So in training, we teach a lot of critical thinking skills. We give members new problems and ask them to think through how they would work out a solution. But site supervisors also have to remember to tell volunteers specific information. And we want site supervisors to refer back to the manuals and to use the information that's there."

Casey consulted with project managers and fellow site supervisors to create a checklist to guide AmeriCorps members through their morning meetings with volunteer groups. Along with Mikey Morris, a fellow two-term AmeriCorps member, Casey has been using the scored checklist with new training methods.

A new member will be called on to be site supervisor of the day, and trainers use the checklist to make sure they hit all the important points of information for the morning meeting. Another scored checklist gauges how well the site supervisor sets goals, motivates volunteers, and uses problem-solving skills. Making sure that every trainee is watched for the same behaviors and judged in the same categories has helped ensure that work sites are more standardized across the organization.

"It's really helped to have two people giving the tutorials and teaching to the checklists," Mikey says. "We can overlap our information and talk to each other about how we're doing. We're always reminding ourselves and them to go back to the site binder, to use the client files and checklists for each phase of construction to make sure we have all the answers."

Some of our talented crew.

It might seem like our drive to standardization is a bit ad hoc. Somebody complains or breaks a foot and gets empowered to make changes. We do not worry about being shoved too far off course because our core values create a clear framework: problem solving, treating work like we are doing it for family, and sharing what we learn. We share the new training methods inside our organization and are starting to share it with others, too. We have begun training AmeriCorps members with our methods and then sending them to other organizations we work with, such as Habitat for Humanity, to spread our approach.

From a retention rate of 72.7% in 2012, we have been moving unsteadily upward. In 2014, it was 77.8%, and in 2015, it was 76.6%. Yes, it is a bit wobbly. With the steady rise in the country's economic conditions, we found that by 2015 we were competing more with higher-paying employers for the best people. But our goals are high, and we are still aiming to retain 85% of AmeriCorps members through their first term.

Standardizing training has benefitted SBP in ways we could not imagine. It has better prepared people for their jobs, yes. But it has also helped us focus on the type of people we need to hire, improved our retention of staff and AmeriCorps members, and helped us define and strengthen our culture. This has been a critical move for SBP as our mission has expanded into new types of interventions and geographic regions. With each new community suddenly thrust into crisis, our ability to offer support brings its own new set of challenges.

Guided by Questions
Expanding Our Mission

On the first Sunday morning in October 2015, the rain had been coming down hard for five days, so people knew that flooding was likely. Dams on private land were failing all over South Carolina. In Columbia, one river after another slopped over its banks, carving new paths through neighborhoods and parks. Cars washed down streets, and bridges let loose with horrible cracking booms.

Johnnie Mae Davis thought she was ready. Snuggled on the couch with her grandchildren, cozy in her brick house, she turned on the news and saw the state Emergency Management Division's warning to stay home and knew it would probably last all day. But that was all right. She had been to the grocery store and planned for the weather. "May as well take a shower now," she said. "We aren't going anywhere."

The hot water wouldn't come on. The water heater wasn't new, but she never had problems with it, so she had to think about where it was. At the top of the basement steps, she peered down into the dark, where everything seemed to be in motion all at once.

It was black water rising. Ms. Davis nearly screamed.

A friend was able to get to a home improvement store and buy a pump, and they set it up as quick as they could. It took seven days to get all the water out of the basement, but since it never crossed the threshold into her house proper, Ms. Davis thought she and her grandchildren, Kelsee and Shamar, were safe. The furnace and hot water heater were ruined, but the house seemed dry.

Then odd things started to happen every day. There would be a damp spot in the middle of the carpet when nothing had spilled and there was no sign of a leak in the ceiling. Tiny black spots appeared high on a couple of walls. She got headaches. The house smelled bad, and she needed to clean the bathroom more often due to the black spots. Her daughter, Latonya, noticed her temper was short, especially when she had been home for a few hours.

Latonya had her own place about 20 minutes away, but she and her young daughter, Rai-vyn, stayed with her mom a lot. The school bus stopped right outside, and it was closer to work. They all liked being together, even if the house suddenly smelled weird.

And then Latonya heard about a little girl—nearly the same age as Rai-vyn—who got an upper-respiratory infection. That girl was airlifted to Atlanta, where she died. Those upper-respiratory infections had been going around her family, too. Ms. Davis and Rai-vyn had already gone to the emergency room for treatment. It was too much. Three weeks after the flood, the two women packed what they could, got the children, and got out. They were luckier than some because Latonya had her own place so they all had somewhere to go, even if it was a lot smaller and farther away from work and school.

Ms. Davis mourned her house as soon as she left. She had bought it with her husband 15 years earlier and had never been late with a mortgage payment. She was proud of paying on time—even through her grief when her husband died just two years after they moved in. Ms. Davis had homeowners insurance, but not flood insurance. It was not required since she did not live in a floodplain. And few people counted on having a 1,000-year rain event like they did in 2015.

As a home health aide, Ms. Davis did not make a lot of money, but she managed. Then the flood and the mold claimed nearly everything she owned: her furniture, her kitchen, her appliances, the furnace, the interior walls of her house and, eventually, every stitch of clothing she owned. Her car survived intact, and that was sheer luck; she could still get herself to work and help out with her grandchildren. Still, the loss was enormous. She cried a lot after the flood and prayed and kept going to work.

Then two of Ms. Davis' elderly clients died, and her work hours were cut. Without her regular income, she was now at risk of losing the house, never mind fixing all the damage. She applied for assistance through FEMA and qualified for about $2,000 to be used for rental housing and $1,700 toward a new furnace. None of that would get her back on her feet. She applied for help through the United Way, and they sent her to an organization that was the official case management agency for FEMA (more on that later), and they sent her to us.

"The SBP folks, they took a look through my house, inspected it all, and just said yes," Ms. Davis says.

That is not the end of the story, of course. After "yes," there is a lot of fundraising, red tape, construction permits to be pulled, calls for new volunteers, and then building. Some of the waiting Ms. Davis encountered is due to waste in SBP processes that we can attack and reduce. And some of the wasted time is baked right into the federal emergency response efforts.[11] We need to attack the wasted time all around because here is one sure fact that we have learned: the further away we get from a disaster's occurrence, the more difficult it is to find volunteers.

11. To be clear, we are using the term "waste" in a technical, but intensely personal, way. Waste means, in this case, unnecessary and avoidable delay. Also, to be clear, there is no judgment in the term, only an opportunity for improvement.

In fact, we ran out of volunteers in Columbia in the late fall of 2016. This was about 14 months after the floods—and just six weeks before Ms. Davis was supposed to have her New Year's Eve homecoming. In late January, she was still waiting to go home.

Waiting and waste are the twin enemies of recovery. They get mixed up together and then magnify each other, becoming a taller and wider barrier standing between Ms. Davis and her cozy brick house. After a disaster, there are always negotiations about who will pay for what. Even after the United States Congress grants funds for relief, money stays at the department of Housing and Urban Development (HUD) for months, as guidelines are written for how funds can be accessed and distributed.

Always, there are procedural hoops for governments and, eventually, homeowners to jump through. Homeowners are usually unprepared to produce the necessary paperwork that is often still somewhere in their ruined houses: title deeds, mortgage papers, and proof of insurance. Lacking the proper paperwork slows recovery. Meanwhile, vulnerable people become more fragile as the weeks, months, even years go on. Too often there is a thin membrane between temporary homelessness and health crises, depression, and additional financial setbacks. Some people who get knocked down cannot get back up again.

Once we started working with Toyota and thinking in terms of root cause analysis to address problems, our discussions about how to help people took new shape. Searching down to the root of the issue, we had to admit that it feels great to welcome home someone like 95-year-old Mr. Lee with cake and a party. But our joy was preceded by his suffering. Shouldn't we work on preventing his suffering in the first place?

Indeed, we discovered an inverse and perverse relationship between how compelling a client is and how long they wait, and then how much credit we get when we finally get people home. The more the client suffered, and the longer, the more appreciation we get. This felt wrong. So, we began asking questions like:

- Why does it take so long to get the most vulnerable people back home?
- Why does rebuilding take so long to finish?
- Why does government funding take so long to arrive?
- Why are people unprepared for disaster?
- Why are governments unprepared?

As anyone can see, there are many roots to follow here. We do not have a single answer. But the discussions did lead us to a few new investigations and conclusions. First, we realized that SBP is not a home-rebuilding organization. Yes, we build and rebuild homes. But that is not what drives us. What drives us is the existential state of people being pushed beyond their means and forced to ask a nonprofit to rebuild their home. That is what motivated us in the first place, to help people like Mr. Andre.

Together with our board, we studied factors that occur after a disaster, that can push people beyond their breaking point. We identified three major causes: time, predictability, and resilience— otherwise known as access to resources. This understanding led to a new mission, shrinking the time between disaster and recovery, and a series of upstream and downstream solutions.

Our goal is for people to get back home before they reach their breaking point. That means the entire snarled root system described in the questions above is our business. The process of disaster recovery, including what happens outside of our organization, is our business. Even preparedness is our business. If we truly care about people like Mr. Lee, we can no longer be willing to reactively ride in at the last moment. Indeed, we need to do all we can to prevent the need for our rebuilding services in the first place.

We bring up this new sense of mission because we want to illustrate where root cause thinking leads, and because we all need to examine the total system of disaster relief more fully. More of us throughout the country are affected every year by extreme weather events or other disasters, natural or man-made. There is a growing possibility that you and we will be on the receiving end of these disaster-relief processes at a most vulnerable time in our lives.

In 2013, 80% of the United States population lived in a county where a federally declared disaster had occurred in the previous nine years.[12] The rate is not slowing. So let's look at how we can improve disaster relief for everyone.

We can start with FEMA. Their very big mission is to "help communities build, sustain, and coordinate delivery of recovery capabilities."[13] In the 20 years between 1996 and 2016, the agency responded to 2,531 natural and man-made disasters, emergency declarations, and fires, from hurricanes to wildfires on unoccupied public lands. The average number of disasters hovers at around 125 annually. In 1997, FEMA responded to 47 disasters; in 2011, the number spiked at 242.

12. "Four Out of Five Americans Live in Areas Hit by Recent Weather Disasters; New Report Says Global Warming to Bring More Extreme Weather," Environment America Research and Policy Center, accessed June 2017, http://environmentamerica.org/news/ame/four-out-five-americans-live-areas-hit-recent-weather-disasters
13. *National Disaster Recovery Framework*, Department of Homeland Security, Second Edition, June 2016. https://www.fema.gov/media-library-data/1466014998123-4bec8550930f774269e0c5968b120ba2/National_Disaster_Recovery_Framework2nd.pdf

Of course, FEMA is not the only government agency responding to disasters. They partner with the Small Business Administration (SBA), to offer low-interest loans to homeowners and businesses in need of funding for repairs. HUD grants money to states and municipalities to rebuild structures destroyed.

The federal agencies have long-standing policies that favor some form of local control of the recovery process. Locally elected or appointed officials—most of whom have little disaster experience—are put in control of large sums of money. Lots of guidelines are imposed to help usher those local officials toward doing the right thing with federal money. Lawyers write those guidelines, mostly in impenetrable language. Local officials all know that if they do not follow the guidelines correctly, hundreds of millions of dollars can be clawed back. People rightly fear having recovery money yanked back, particularly when their city or state is in the midst of economic peril.

Paralysis can also easily set in and not just locally. Following a disaster, a state usually requests funds from Congress. If Congress approves, a request is sent to HUD to administer funds. Here a pile of money typically sits while officials do their best to balance compliance with regulations with lessons learned from past disasters. Meanwhile, Ms. Davis is driving her grandchildren to and from the bus stop every day, hoping her car survives without need of repair, and trying to find affordable clothes to replace everyone's winter gear. Every day is a struggle in cramped conditions.

In the disaster zone, FEMA officials direct local officials to set up a Long-Term Recovery Committee. The committee facilitates meetings between local officials—or their designees—and the various recovery agencies. FEMA also designates one or several groups as the official Disaster Case Management organization. Their mandate is to be responsible for connecting people in need with organizations like SBP that receive public and private funds and usually operate on a statewide basis.

We have attended sessions of Long-Term Recovery Committees in five states and have found them to be stuck balancing urgency and fidelity to long-held processes. Disaster case management groups usually need to maintain a certain-sized caseload in order to meet contract requirements. Our preference would be for contracts to incentivize outputs—clients who achieve success—as opposed to case load. In our first 16 months of rebuilding in Louisiana, working outside of the official emergency management channels, we completed rebuilding on 88 houses. In that same time period, the Long-Term Recovery Committee working in St. Bernard Parish had identified—but not yet distributed—funds to complete 13 houses.

By funneling millions of dollars through a case-management agency, FEMA has set up a classic case of batch processing. People in need must all be funneled through the narrow capacity of the case manager. The process all takes place within a black box; there is no transparency. At the end of an often-lengthy application process for the disaster victims, relief organizations like SBP usually receive, at best, just the name and phone number of a person in need. The information we receive is not always accurate, and our clients almost always need to repeat the process with us.

Citizens and governments suffer from the same lack of preparedness. People come out of a disaster without the necessary paperwork to prove home ownership. Most have not looked at their insurance coverage for years. Governments often run drills simulating the first hours and days of a major disaster. They practice medical triage and set up systems to coordinate with utilities to get services back up. But the forward-looking does not usually extend past about a week, and certainly not to thinking about how to efficiently get the most vulnerable citizens back home.

Our Five Interventions

After working with Toyota advisors for about a year and feeling the freedom that comes from having more reliable operations—meaning we spent less time firefighting every day—we began investigating how to attack some of these bigger issues. We identified five areas that, if left unaddressed, lead to a delayed, unpredictable, and unsatisfactory recovery. We organized them into five categories: rebuild, share, prepare, advise, and advocate.

For each of these categories, we created interventions designed to improve the work. They are direct responses to the questions that came up in our root cause inquiries. These five interventions are larger, long-term projects that are taking SBP into new directions. They constitute the path we take to shrink the time between disaster and recovery.

I. Rebuild houses in an innovative way

This encompasses much of the process improvement work we do on a regular basis. It is a promise that we will continue to push ourselves toward creative processes and building techniques. This includes work like standardizing plumbing rough-ins to improve scheduling predictability and allow apprentices to do the work while supervised, or developing panelized construction for interior and exterior walls using jigs[14] so that volunteers can build good walls in four minutes or less without training and with less waste.

A great example of this panelized construction took place at the Farmers Insurance Open in 2018. This is a PGA Tour event in La Jolla, California, where 30 executives from Farmers Insurance built all the wall panels for three houses in one hour. After two

---

14. Jigs are devices that hold a piece of work and guide the tools operating on it.

hours of loading (lots of room for process improvement here), UPS shipped the wall panels to New Orleans. There, in three hours, a different team of Farmers employees erected the walls for a house.

Knowing the powerful impact this work has had on our costs and predictability, we continue to look for more areas in which we can introduce innovative techniques and make them standardized work. In the future, we are working toward building sites that do not create excess waste. The zero-landfill job site is on the horizon.

Further, we've applied our constructive discontent to multi-family residential affordable housing for veterans and seniors. In December 2018, SBP will break ground on a 50-unit development for veterans and seniors that will be the first net-zero affordable housing development in the South. Support from Entergy, the local utility, and Toyota will make this project possible.

A row of new SBP-built homes.

2. Share: Train others in our methods

Another thing we learned from Toyota and deeply internalized is that simply improving our own processes is not enough. Toyota uses the term *yokoten*, which to us means, "If you do it well, share it." This idea resonates with us. In fact, Zack annoys SBP staff and Toyota team members alike with his commitment to crank yokoten up to "yokotwenty."

Recalling one of our core values—do your work the way you would want it done for your grandparents—we realized that if our loved ones needed their home rebuilt, we would not care which organization, wearing which shirt, did the work. We would simply want the work done in a prompt, efficient, and predictable manner. This is what the share intervention intends to achieve: increase capacity and efficiency in the nonprofit rebuilding industry, to increase the chances that anyone's loved ones would get the support they need.

We started this sharing in 2014, by gathering the resources we had in-house and, with a generous grant and guidance from our corporate partner Farmers Insurance, wrote *The Disaster Recovery Playbook*. Intended both for communities trying to recover from disaster and for other relief agencies looking to help them, the playbook details considerations for goal-setting after disaster, as well as specific steps and approaches to meet those goals.

For instance, organizations that choose process goals that focus on how work is done instead of outcome goals that measure results risk becoming mired in the details of their own work, at the expense of speedy recovery for clients. The idea behind the playbook was that anyone could pick it up and start a rebuilding effort, using everything we have learned through trial-and-error over a decade.

Information in the *Disaster Recovery Playbook* covers:

- Launching a non-profit rebuilding program in 10 steps
- Managing volunteers
- Case management: how to assist clients, step-by-step
- Development: how to raise money, including use of social media
- Construction: managing a volunteer-driven construction company
- Systems: whiteboards, project management, etc.

After the South Carolina floods in 2015 and Hurricane Harvey hit Houston, Texas, in 2017, we expanded our yokoten services. In South Carolina, we partnered with the state and several funders, including the United Way of the Midlands, to share SBP's systems, processes, and AmeriCorps members with a number of independent rebuilding organizations. All with the goal of helping them reach scale and achieve efficiency.

In communities hit by Hurricane Harvey, we rolled out this intervention with greater force. With generous funding from the Greater Houston Community Foundation and an increased allocation of AmeriCorps members from the Corporation for National and Community Service, we've provided mold remediation, gutting, and case management training to more than 50 organizations. We also invested AmeriCorps members in seven different NGOs.

We feel that SBP's share work honors Mr. Lee's legacy—the world would have been much better if any group, not just SBP, rebuilt Mr. Lee's house sooner.

3. Prepare: Individualized resilience and recovery training

For most people, getting back home was complicated by the fact that they were unprepared. We had seen the results of this over and over again. Much existing training focuses on evacuation and protecting physical safety. To be sure, this is crucial. But here we identified a gap: people need to know what they can do to protect their property and to maximize resources after disaster.

In 2014, we decided to try new ways to get upstream of our operations and help people prepare for a disaster. As part of a three-year grant from Zurich, the global insurance and risk management company and one of our corporate partners, we focused on changing behaviors before disaster strikes in order to expedite recovery.

We chose 10 communities around the country that were diverse in size, make up, and risk and applied targeted training for residents and small businesses. We were fortunate to hire a young woman, Autumn Lotze from the Red Cross National Headquarters community mobilization and partnership team. Well versed in the needs and difficulties of creating prepared communities, Autumn hit the ground running and has not stopped.

Using a phased rollout over 14 months, Autumn and colleagues approached each new community with a similar agenda. First, they connected with the existing emergency management infrastructure. Most cities have such an office, where they could meet and collect information on what the city had tried as far as preparedness and what had or had not worked.

Then, Autumn identified the groups that might yield more information or would be able to pull together groups of people for one-hour training classes. These groups included school districts, universities, financial aid and literacy programs, chambers of commerce, and large or mid-sized companies.

Large employers, such as Toyota in San Antonio, Texas, could set up a series of lunchtime meetings with employees. With smaller companies, Autumn usually had more luck getting in through industry or civic associations or unions. In many small and mid-sized companies, giving up an hour for free preparedness training was a hard sell. But in nearly every community, she found unexpected venues through word-of-mouth, such as exercise groups, book clubs, or addiction support meetings.

Every class covered five main topics in a curriculum based on our experiences and put together in partnership with Zurich. The class covers 1) how to identify and stay informed about local risks; 2) emergency and continuity planning; 3) getting proper insurance coverage and protecting important documents; 4) how to work the system in the aftermath; and 5) creating physical improvements to a home or business to increase safety. Each person who attended the one-hour resilience training received a preparedness checklist, a resource guide with more information, a list of websites for various information sources, and a list of local resources.

The best test of how well the resilience training works would be if twin disasters hit one of our targeted communities and a nearby community that had received no training. This did not happen, of course, nor would we wish it. Instead, we depended on surveys.

Of the 3,000 people who attended training within the first 12 months, a full 98% reported learning something new in surveys taken directly after the session. And 93% said they intended to take action. The trouble is with follow-up. Our three-month-later surveys have been met with less interest, with a response rate of just 3%–5%. Of those who replied, 75% said they had taken some steps to prepare for trouble. The response rate is too low, however, to be significant.

From this project, we learned that we need more engagement with people over time. A single one-hour class is not enough. We need to find more channels to send our message, more ways to engage people. We have learned that people who have been touched by disaster in some way are receptive to training, but for others the concept of catastrophe is an abstraction.

With discontent at our ability to scale impact, SBP is embarking on two new endeavors. First, with support from the Walmart Foundation and Farmers Insurance, we are seeking to increase subscriptions to flood insurance using a digital media campaign.

If we want people fortified against their breaking point, one way to do this is to increase their vertical resilience (e.g., access to resources). Getting more people to buy flood insurance has a powerful impact. Two important facts: 1) in Houston after Harvey, nearly 80% of impacted houses were located in zones where flood insurance was not required, and 2) the average annual cost of a $250,000 flood insurance policy was $850 a year.

We tested this flood insurance promotion program in Louisiana. In three months and for less than $10,000, we reached more than 200,000 homeowners; 7,000 watched a short video on flood insurance; and 4,000 downloaded an e-book. We imagine that many of them subsequently bought flood insurance. With further support from Farmers, we are targeting eight new communities in 2019.

Our second share strategy to reach scaled impact addresses the inherent limitations of preparedness training programs. Autumn's compelling, no doubt, but there are built-in limitations to training that requires people to sit in a room (or at their computer) for a 30–45-minute presentation. We heard from many of our customers, employers who saw value in our training, that they simply couldn't have their employees attend a long training session.

With that in mind, and with support from Zurich, Walmart, and Farmers, SBP is building an e-learning platform, designed to address two goals: help people to gain resources and help them to avoid squandering them. The platform has videos and personalized learning focused on flood insurance, document retention, avoiding contractor fraud, navigating FEMA, and understanding the truth about mold.

We believe that knowledge is power, and with knowledge, people can position themselves positively in relation to one of the key factors tied to breaking point: predictability.

4. Advise: Work with government agencies to lay a better foundation for recovery

By 2013, we had been involved in the early stages of a disaster in four states. We had resources freed up by more reliable operations, and we were increasingly worried. From these conditions, we launched another new initiative: SBP's Disaster Recovery Lab.

In the immediate aftermaths of Hurricane Katrina, the Joplin tornado, flooding in Texas, and Superstorm Sandy, we saw federal aid get stalled in bureaucracy and a lot of money—tens of millions of dollars—being spent on major consulting firms that offered states and cities guidance in how to get and keep HUD money. We saw disadvantaged people being pressured into forced mortgage payoffs, when banks captured their clients' insurance payouts and compelled them to use the money to pay off or pay down mortgage debts instead of repairing damage. And we saw a lot of contractor fraud.

People needed information and a game plan much earlier in the process. We created the Disaster Recovery Lab in order to devote time to finding ways to intervene earlier. Out of that, the *Disaster Recovery Playbook* was created. The playbook is a good resource, but we wanted to back up words with action. We wanted to know how we could make the recovery in Joplin work as well in month four as New Orleans was running in year six.

Reese May was one of the people who helped lay the foundation. You may remember Reese from our work after Superstorm Sandy (see page 30). When we first met Reese, he was taking a break from graduate studies in philosophy and recouping from two tours in Iraq with the Marines. A Mississippi native, he was living in the mid-city area of New Orleans, thinking he would bartend for a year of fun. But during long afternoon runs through his neighborhood, he was shocked by the number of houses still boarded up and sinking slowly back into the earth. So he joined AmeriCorps, became an SBP construction coordinator, and worked closely with Liz.

It was soon apparent that Reese's critical thinking skills and can-do attitude made him a valuable asset. As our needs in construction became less pressing, he began talking about returning

Reese May (left) being recognized by the Red Cross for work in NY/NJ.

to his studies at the University of Mississippi. But we had other ideas. We talked him out of his dream of becoming a professor of philosophy—for now—and got him tackling difficult problems. Like, how can we take all the lessons we have learned and apply real solutions in a way that people will hear? How can we get municipal governments and agencies better prepared to help people to become recovery experts?

"I will tell you one thing, and that is nobody is offering real, unvarnished lessons-learned from one disaster to another," Reese says. "Nikki Haley [former governor of South Carolina, Republican] is not calling up Chuck Schumer [senior senator of New York, Democrat] to ask for recovery advice or offer tips. That just does not happen. And disaster recovery has no national associations, no trade unions to guide people."

SBP volunteers in South Carolina.

Someone needed to fill that role. In the *Disaster Recovery Playbook* we offer a step-by-step guide to creating local or statewide recovery organizations to maximize federal funding. But human contact is better than a book for guiding state and local leaders through the thicket of rules and needs. So, from the beginning of South Carolina's flooding and recovery effort, Reese and Zack were there, meeting with state leaders and helping to pass along the best practices we had learned.

J.R. Sanderson, another combat veteran, was the program management director of the South Carolina disaster recovery office. He focused on the impact of policy decisions on human beings and was a careful and exacting steward of public money. He was Reese and Zack's main contact and shared many of our concerns from the beginning. He listened intently as they talked about the problems SBP had seen in other states, such as millions of dollars diverted to big-name consulting firms and process redundancies that slowed recovery to a crawl. When recovery slows, people lose heart and leave the area, undermining the tax base and sometimes sending towns into insolvency.

"We built an entire transcontinental railway in six years. It shouldn't take us 10 years to recover from a flood," says J.R.

South Carolina still needed consultants to help deal with federal regulations, so J.R. rewrote the formal Request for Proposal (RFP) such that the winning group would be paid based on outcomes and output, instead of by the hour. This cut the consulting bill and made it knowable. Then the state started to attack the waste in the initial phases of recovery, before the first sheets of drywall can be hung, what J.R. calls the "flash-to-bang" time lag.

Traditionally, states have hired case managers to go house-to-house and collect information—on paper—about the citizens who need help, recording who owns what, who needs what, and the extent of damage. That information then goes to an implementation vendor that ensures eligibility for federal funds. These two private companies were individually contracted by the state, and the information handoff was not smooth or quick. Disaster victims were always asked to take all the information they already gave to the case manager and deliver it again to the implementation vendor.

J.R. wanted to cut out some of the middle-management waste. He thought maybe they could in-source some of that work. Zack talked him through the process of pulling together an in-house case management team. With its own team, South Carolina will be able to collect information directly from citizens about needs and damage, prioritize those needs based on vulnerability, and feed the data directly into the implementation vendor's system. Vendors can then make focused requests for any additional documentation. Then a team, including a construction subcontractor, will be sent out to houses to collect missing information and get real construction estimates all at once. J.R. calls this the "one-knock method."

With Reese's encouragement, J.R. also tapped into a state nonprofit recovery fund set up by Governor Haley, to hire AmeriCorps teams to do the early muck-and-gut work on flooded houses. He says, "We got through the mucking and gutting a lot faster than we had before."

The result of this work, still in its early stages as of this writing, is encouraging. After the 2015 floods, 15 months passed between the inundation and the beginning of reconstruction on the first homes. J.R.'s improved system cut that flash-to-bang time to 11 months after Hurricane Matthew hit in October 2016. As unpaid, third-party advisors, we are helping where we can—including training South Carolina's first cohort of in-house case managers.

Zack helping to assess the situation in Baton Rouge in 2016.

Using the South Carolina intervention as a model, we are working to assist other states. When a massive rainstorm caused flooding in Baton Rouge in 2016, we used some of Reese's methods to engage Louisiana's recovery leadership. In Houston, we worked with the city government to think through strategies to speed arrival and reduce barriers to getting disaster funds directly to homeowners. In both cases, we saw the states trying out new ideas, such as putting together rebuilding teams, accepting bids for work, and even using private-bank bridge loans to begin construction before government appropriations arrived—a small risk up-front for a huge time savings between disaster destruction and the first hammer swing.

Going forward, we will focus some of these efforts on a few initiatives, including better, faster data collection. Presently, FEMA relies on those house-to-house, paper surveys taken by inspectors in the days—sometimes weeks—after a disaster. The damage reports could be collected faster and more accurately with a few more tools, such as drones, GPS, and satellite data while the water is still high.

Reese is also working on developing prebuilt action plans to help states and cities access HUD funds faster. The number of disaster types is small, and the facts of our physical world do not change all that often. We imagine being able to create documents for hurricanes, river flooding, tornadoes, earthquakes, large fires, or acts of terrorism that are ready to be populated by data and customized to the needs of government programs and to subsequent rebuilding efforts.

We are pushing for these changes with the firm belief that we can make the response of SBP, governments, and agencies more predictable and more efficient. We have found that people can hang on and wait awhile for help. But they can stay stronger and wait longer if they know when help is coming. Predictability is key.

5. Advocate: Measure what matters

There is a favorite saying among engineers: "You are what you measure." This is a reflection of the fact that what we measure becomes the focus of our attention, our improvement efforts, and even the definition of our organizations.

If we measure how many bottles of water we deliver to disaster victims, for instance, innovation energy becomes focused on how to move that number upward. We compete with others on who delivers the most water; we start to think of ourselves as water suppliers. This is simply human nature.

This is why the fifth focus of our advocacy begins with the mantra "Measure what matters." We want the numbers to reflect human welfare. We want states and agencies to measure how quickly people are returned to permanent housing, not just how many dollars are spent or how many partnerships are created with community and religious groups. In other words, we want people to measure outcomes.

We push for governments and major relief agencies to set clear goals and then measure outcomes to create standardized, repeatable processes. We have seen repeatedly that people hit their breaking points when they do not know how long their misery will last. Months after all of their possessions have melted into a moldy mess and their mortgage holder has begun threatening foreclosure, if they still see no end in sight, that's when people give up, break down, and fall off the recovery road.

If we truly want to help, we must be committed to offering a helping hand that is reliable. Being reliable means having standardized, repeatable work processes, not reinventing the wheel every time there's a flood.

A focus on measuring what matters can even lead to legislative fixes. In 2016, we began working on various pieces of legislation that we hope will gain traction in state houses and Congress. For instance, one piece of legislation would allow people to indicate on their tax returns that FEMA can be granted access to IRS information regarding home ownership, insurance, and income in cases of a federally declared disaster. This would allow FEMA to access secure, existing information even when all a homeowner's papers have been destroyed.

SBP supporter JJ Watt (right) with a client family in Houston.

Doing Well to Do Good

None of us can do this alone. The big storms are becoming more frequent and more destructive. In just five months in 2016, there were 1,000-year floods in Maryland, Louisiana, West Virginia, and Texas.[15] When Hurricane Harvey struck Houston in August 2017, it was on the heels of two 500-year floods the two previous years.

Harvey made a mockery of Houston's flood-zone maps.[16] It lingered over the coastline, dumping some 30 inches of rain on the greater Houston area, while high winds and lashing rain leveled several blocks in nearby Rockport on the Gulf Coast. One hundred and three people died and 13,000 required rescue. The Texas Department of Public Safety counted 185,000 homes damaged and 9,000 destroyed.

SBP arrived in Texas five days after the storm. Cliona Roberts, a graduate of Tulane University whom everyone calls Cli, was an executive director of SBP's operations in Baton Rouge. When we asked her to lead our post-Harvey recovery efforts, she hopped in her car and headed for Texas. She dropped off an AmeriCorps member in Houston and kept driving down to Rockport. There she found herself standing in the middle of a devastated town, surrounded by miles of human misery.

15. A 1,000-year flood has a one in 1,000 chance of occurring in a given year. Likewise, a 500-year flood has a one in 500 probability.
16. Nearly 75% of damaged homes were outside the FEMA designated mandatory flood insurance zone; most of those homeowners were uninsured against high water. David Hunn, Matt Dempsey, and Mihir Zaveri, "Harvey's Floods," *The Houston Chronicle*, March 30, 2018.

Cli knew that SBP could reliably rebuild about 100 homes in a year. That's our rule-of-thumb time frame for every area in which we set up full operations.

"It is incredibly daunting when you think about it," Cli says. "How are 100 homes going to help, out of something like 200,000 houses damaged or destroyed? A good portion of those homeowners can help themselves. Some will qualify for help through the city or county. Some will move. The rest are ours, and there are thousands of them."

As Cli went about setting up a local organization to start rebuilding, she was also thinking about SBP's five types of intervention. Her job was to rebuild, but it was also to share, prepare, advise, and advocate. This is the best way we know to expand our impact broader than those first 100 families.

Cli reached out to other disaster management organizations, like Habitat for Humanity and United Way. We offered help in creating client case management services, introducing more efficient rebuilding operations, attracting volunteers, and sharing information about funding sources.

When we had clients in need of very expensive repairs, we partnered with Habitat for Humanity to share the costs. For seven organizations that struggled with client case management—and this is common, since every homeowner qualifies for some programs but not others, and prioritizing their needs is difficult—we embedded our SBP-trained AmeriCorps case managers in their operations.

Team Rubicon

One great example of a partnership that was created in those early days after Hurricane Harvey was with Team Rubicon. Team Rubicon is a veteran-led, international disaster response organization made up of military veterans, first responders, and civilians focused on helping people who are overlooked or underserved by traditional aid efforts in disaster zones. It is an incredible group.

Beginning in 2010 following the earthquake in Haiti, Team Rubicon became experts in early disaster response—conducting damage assessments, clearing debris, mucking and gutting homes, making expedient home repairs—largely by repurposing the energy and skills of veterans who still wanted to serve outside of combat after they hung up their uniforms.

Team Rubicon on the ground in Houston.

Cli was impressed with how hard Team Rubicon worked and how much they got done. But they were always leaving hard-hit areas within a few months—mission complete—even though team members got invested in communities and many wanted to stay to assist with longer-term recovery. So, SBP started to talk with their leaders about creating a sustained rebuilding effort. It was a big shift for their mission, but it was an opportunity the group had been looking for.

"There was always a thought, in the brief history of Team Rubicon," says Ken Farris, former army officer and construction manager for Team Rubicon in Houston, "that there was a missing piece of our recovery work. We received so many donations after Harvey, we finally had the financial means to put together a long-term recovery and rebuilding program."

Ken had worked in construction for 20 years before joining Team Rubicon. After Hurricane Ike hit Texas in 2008 and tore the roof off his family home, Ken and his wife replaced it themselves, along with all of their interior walls. He knew how to build. But doing it with volunteers instead of subcontractors meant providing everyone with all the tools and training to do the work. Every week. On every job.

It was an extra layer of organization that was difficult to think through. But Cli showed Ken how to put together supplies and tools in kits and how SBP trained volunteers on site. We embedded an SBP-trained AmeriCorps case manager in their operations, who set up a client-tracking whiteboard showing every phase of the client applications. Team Rubicon began their long-term rebuilding efforts with a small team and swung their first hammers inside a house in March 2018. They have a goal of completing work on 100 houses by the end of 2020.

For all the fresh hope Cli encountered in Houston, there were some old problems too. A Long-Term Recovery Committee was set up, and FEMA selected a group to do case management for people in need. There were more than a dozen rebuilding organizations anxious to get cases and start work. But referrals just weren't making it out of the case management group. This is not a new story in disaster zones.

Meanwhile, money was pouring into Houston, in donations large and small from people throughout the world. Harris County Judge Ed Emmett and Houston Mayor Sylvester Turner set up a Hurricane Harvey Relief Fund within the Greater Houston Community Foundation and raised more than $115 million in 14 months.

JJ Watt, defensive end for the NFL's Houston Texans, spent much of the 2017 season off the field with an injury and raising money for disaster relief. Beginning with $100,000 of his own money, his fund quickly grew to $37 million.

In October 2017, JJ told us he would announce that $8.5 million would be granted to SBP's rebuilding efforts. We knew this announcement would create a lot of interest, so we immediately created an application for assistance and put it on our website. Within three days, 1,000 homeowners had applied. We learned a lot from this experience. Suddenly, we had direct access to people who needed us, instead of waiting for case management programs to hire, train, and scale up or waiting on long-term recovery committees to form and deliver consistent results. In our haste, however, we did not ask for enough information, particularly regarding insurance, FEMA eligibility, and income.

While we worked to correct our error, the Greater Houston Community Foundation and its consultants saw that we had acted quickly and had a lot of experience. While other organizations were

JJ Watt (center) with a team in Houston.

applying for grants to begin working on specific areas or houses, the Greater Houston foundation asked SBP to take over relief efforts in four underserved zip codes in southeast Houston. Then, Hurricane Harvey Relief Fund managers asked that SBP partner with them on a simplified application process called Harvey Home Connect.

In the four months between June and October 2018 (the latest information we have, as of this writing) we had processed almost 1,000 applications for repair and referred those cases out to the 15 rebuilding groups still operating in Texas. People got to work.

Puerto Rico

Meanwhile, Hurricane Maria ripped through Puerto Rico in late September, just two weeks after Hurricane Irma had hit the island. Maria was the deadliest storm of the 2017 season, killing at least 3,057 people. The electric grid failed. Seventy percent of the island's drinking water was not safe to drink in the weeks after the storm.

We sent a small team to Puerto Rico as soon as we could and were introduced to the logistical nightmare of rebuilding on an island without a working infrastructure. Building supplies were hard to come by and expensive. The island is split in half by a mountain range. Roads leading out of population centers quickly became steep dirt tracks.

We have learned a lot over the years about the importance of local knowledge. We need to understand our clients, as well as area rules and customs. So we were happy to connect with an old friend, Jordan Sanchez.

Jordan is a graduate of Rutgers University, where he studied economics. He worked in banking and then with the Clinton Global Initiative in disaster response and resilience, managing sponsor relationships. And he had already worked with us, helping to expand our AmeriCorps program before Hurricane Maria hit.

But really, Jordan was involved in Puerto Rico even before his time at SBP. He and his cousin Jeff Moran-Morales began an initiative to share the real stories of survivors in Puerto Rico after the storm. Their grandparents are from Puerto Rico, and both grew up with a strong sense of Puerto Rican identity.

They called on each other to serve after Hurricane Maria. With Jeff's background as a documentarian, they hit on the idea of telling survivor stories to highlight the individual experiences that get lost within the dominant narrative. They created content, found partners

Jordan Sanchez (second from left) with a client family in Puerto Rico.

on the ground, built a website, and used social media to connect survivors with needed resources.

Eight months later, Jordan handed off that work to Jeff and accepted a job with SBP as its new executive director in Puerto Rico. He took stock of the work ahead. There were about 330,000 buildings damaged, with 20% in need of full rebuilding. There were more than 200 organizations registered as doing rebuilding work, but there was little communication between the groups.

Jordan established an office with five staff members—all island residents—and went about recruiting another 21 AmeriCorps members. All of them were local, too. Our warehouse manager in

New Orleans set up asset management and warehouse tracking systems and trained the new team. An SBP finance team helped staff create dashboards and reporting mechanisms. And a team from SBP New Jersey taught Jordan's team production management.

Normally, we would have started Jordan's team making prefab walls with volunteers, but most of the island's houses were made of concrete. They really needed roof repair and interior finishing. So, Jordan's team first rewrote the construction staging process and created new work kits. With his team of local talent, they also began navigating the building and permitting laws, which, like in the rest of the US, change from one town to the next. Then they figured out how to manage the mix of clients into small and medium jobs and complete rebuilds.

Almost all of the medium-size jobs and the rebuilds needed roofs. As in the mainland US, this was not something that could be assigned to volunteers. Fortunately, Team Rubicon was also working in Puerto Rico and had decided to specialize in roofs. Using a small staff and large donations, Team Rubicon hired a group of local roofers and got to work.[17] In late 2018, the team was finishing a steady 18 roofs every week. We partnered with them on most of our jobs, and they pulled us in when they come across clients who needed interior work but could not afford a contractor.

Other groups like the Carlos Beltran Foundation, Ricky Martin Foundation, and United Methodists are also important partners in Puerto Rico. They have long-term local relationships, a deep knowledge of community needs, and financial resources. Working together with these groups, we are on track to finish 100 homes in our first 12 months in Puerto Rico.

17. In conversation with donors, Team Rubicon decided to hire local roofers—thus injecting money into the local economy—rather than paying to fly volunteers and Team Rubicon members to the island.

We kept pushing forward, even as new hurricanes in 2018 sent us to fresh disasters in the Carolinas and Florida. For the fourth year in a row, storm activity began early, well before the official June 1 start of the hurricane season. Florence was the wettest hurricane on record in North Carolina, causing $16.7 billion in damage. Overall losses for the 2018 hurricane season were estimated to be $31 billion, $14 billion of which was uninsured.[18]

Thinking about the money tied up in disaster response can be overwhelming. But it is the human impact that drives us to improve. In every storm there are deaths and disrupted lives. Disasters can push previously independent and self-sufficient people to their breaking point, especially when they face a long and unpredictable recovery, with no clear path forward, and without understanding if or how they can access resources. Many people can bounce back, but others cannot—especially people who work hard yet live at the edge of their means.

Creating a world of resilience where people will never need to turn to SBP or other such groups is what drives us forward. People at risk of being pushed beyond their breaking point is what drives our theory of change. We have learned that after a disaster there are three big levers driving outcomes: time, predictability, and access to resources. Beyond rebuilding houses, this is where we must make our biggest bets. And this is why our five interventions exist.

We will always rebuild. But it is the four other interventions that allow us to expand our reach and truly reduce the time between disaster and recovery. It is what we would want for our loved ones and what communities across our country deserve.

18. Munich Re puts damage estimates at $31 billion for North America, almost all of which occurred in the United States. https://www.munichre.com/topics-online/en/ climate-change-and-natural-disasters/natural-disasters/storms/ hurricanes-and-typhoons-2018.html

Training other NGOs to use SBP's model allows us to increase the number of people served. Helping hundreds of thousands of homeowners to get the right insurance before disaster, to access—and not lose—FEMA aid, insurance benefits, and HUD resources after disaster, adds predictability and significantly increases access to resources. Working with states and cities to structure large-scale procurement so that contracts favor citizens, measure outputs, and set clear deadlines speeds recovery. Helping to bring to the federal government the same house-by-house damage assessment technology used by national insurance companies also adds predictability and reduces time.

The bigger storms and ever-widening need leave us despondent and energized in equal measure. Climate change is a human-powered catastrophe that destroys more lives every year. The science on this is clear. And yet, we find hope in the fact that our work has shown that we can and should believe in people. At every turn, we have seen people leap into action, putting their time and dollars on the line, putting their bodies in the way to save others.

We have to believe that we can correct course and avert the larger disasters. We have seen that humanity runs deeper than political affiliation. No volunteer has ever asked the political party of one of our clients; no donor has ever asked that we operate in a red city or a blue town. At times of need, what unites us proves far stronger than what could divide us.

SBP seeks to utilize this human compulsion to help others to ensure that America's system of resilience and recovery is commensurate not just with need, but with our true potential. We work hard to ensure resilience before disaster and to shape behaviors so that people can access and keep resources after disaster.

Looking back through our story, it is the human capacity for change that gives us hope. We were two people with no experience in building houses or creating a national organization, and we made a difference. Anyone can be that difference, given the will and a lot of help from others. As the parents of a young child, we know that our son's future rests on this faith we have in our capacity for change. The futures of all our children and grandchildren do.

Starting Tomorrow

How can you apply these improvement methods to your own organization? This book exists because we believe that this philosophy and these tools can fundamentally change any group for the better. We are committed to sharing them whenever and wherever we can. We believe that any charity, corporation, or government entity can use TPS to better fulfill its mission.

First, leaders need to recognize the noise and waste that lies between their intentions and actual outcomes. If this feels overwhelming, begin the change with a few useful tools. Improving your operations is an easier place to start than talking about big issues like organizational culture. This is how we teach others to begin.

Whiteboards

Making work visible for all was our biggest game changer. Simply making sure that everyone has a common understanding of today's work and being able to see daily goals at a glance was a revelation for us.

A lot of people want to digitize this process, to create computer files and put them on a public server. But this requires that people go and retrieve these files. It's better to have big, public boards that people can gather around for a morning meeting. Many voices in the process make for shared understanding. Look at your goals together and ask: What is standing in the way of getting our mission accomplished today?

A big part of this work is creating deadlines and accountability. Deadlines can be a scary word. But you need to have a communal understanding of what you mean to do and by when. Only with deadlines can you initiate conversations about why important work did not happen, what barriers stood in the way, and how to knock down those barriers.

A common method for solving problems

We teach our people to work through the following seven problem-solving steps together:

1. Go see the problem at the point of occurrence.
2. Collect facts (a record of events) and data (measurements of those events) regarding the problem.
3. Set a future target condition and date for completion.
4. Perform root cause analysis using the 5 *Whys*.
5. Analyze the factors involved, including the people, the materials or machines, and the methods used.
6. Analyze the proposed countermeasures for effects on the organization.
7. Create a plan: who does what, when, in order to put the countermeasures in place?

When everyone knows the step-by-step method of getting to a root cause and creating countermeasures, addressing problems becomes a much simpler process. At SBP, we know that the first step is going to the site of the problem and observing it. It's like hunting nutria—you need to see a problem in its natural environment to understand it. During this phase it is important to reiterate that people are not at fault, the process is.

Then we use the 5 Whys inquiry method to drill down further into the issues. This stops us from stabbing around wildly and rushing to solutions. Using the information gleaned from seeing the process in its natural environment, we analyze the issue from four perspectives: man, machine, method, and materials. We ask what people did, how machines or the supply of materials affected the work, and whether our methods—the work processes—were effective.

Finally, we propose countermeasures. This includes who will do what and when. Again, we include deadlines and accountability to ensure that everyone is clear on what they will deliver. We are respectful of people while making these deadlines, always asking when someone can reasonably deliver their piece of the counter-measure, and what kind of assistance they might need, instead of arbitrarily assigning a date.

We have seen in our own organization that having a common problem-solving method takes a lot of the emotion out of a process that can otherwise seem like an attempt to cast blame.

Standardized work

We have taught quite a few rebuilding organizations about TPS and have found that our site binders really capture their attention. These are the three-ring binders filled with everything from dry-wall hanging instructions, to checklists for conducting morning meetings with volunteers, to the personal story of the family that owns the home. This is not like the standardized work you find in a factory—it is not strict, step-by-step, timed, and synchronized tasks. But this is a level of organization and instruction that other volunteer-driven rebuilders just don't have. (See examples on pages 129–135.)

Building on their interest in the site binders, we talk about the real power of standardization: knowing how long jobs will take. And once we know the standard work of a plumbing rough-in, for instance, we can teach that job to others. Assistants can do the work, overseen by a licensed plumber who can now be working on multiple jobs at once. After years of being told that construction was never standard and time lines were implausible, we have found that we can actually assign time frames to most jobs. We can write out the steps and teach the work more easily to our ever-changing crews.

Seeing these tools in action—whiteboards, common problem solving, and standardized work—gets a lot of organizations hooked on the possibilities. That's when we can talk about the necessary cultural changes and how a new mind-set can free people to reimagine their work.

Imagine creating an environment in your organization in which problems are embraced as learning opportunities. Visualize congratulating colleagues on uncovering sticky issues and creating excitement around finding their root cause. Think of all the waste you encounter as a barrier between you and achieving your mission—which is the reason you started your organization, the reason you show up every day. And once you start addressing problems, removing waste, and creating better processes, visualize having the courage and discipline to embrace standardization.

Along the way, the role of a leader will change. Founders and CEOs who embrace TPS find that they are no longer the lone deciders. Instead, they become coaches and mentors, helping people find and address problems, and discovering the creative strength of everyone. It means giving up some authorship of your organization's success because it belongs to everyone.

We know this is a humbling experience. It can be hard and scary to let go of the reins. But there is a freedom that comes from admitting that you do not have all the answers. As leaders of an organization, we know the pressure that we once put on ourselves to answer everyone's questions. We really did think we were supposed to know everything. When we shifted our focus to respecting the knowledge and experience of others, to letting others lead us toward becoming a better organization, we found untapped talents and an incredible source of creative energy.

Success has many definitions. A lot of people think that TPS methods are all about going faster and getting more productivity out of your people and processes. However, going faster and increased productivity are not so much goals as they are by-products of removing waste in the system and addressing problems. The goal of this work is really to better understand and execute to mission, to respect people by giving them tools to solve problems, and to embrace the struggle of ongoing improvement.

Doing this work will change you. It changed us. We worked hard to learn our construction skills, and we are proud of them. But we also put a priority on teaching other organizations to use TPS to build better and faster, because success for us is not how many houses SBP builds. Success is shrinking the time between disaster and recovery for as many people as possible, to get everyone home.

Doing Well to ...

ON SITE
CONSTRUCTION MANUAL

Shrinking the time between disaster and recovery

TABLE OF CONTENTS

IMPORTANT CONTACT INFORMATION

OFFICE NUMBERS NOLA

Main Office	504-277-6831
Construction Office	504-343-7291
Client Services Office	504-644-4639 ext 104
Volunteer Services Office	504-302-9190 ext 107
Warehouse	504-251-7818

PROJECT MANAGERS (PM)

ROLE OF THE PROJECT MANAGER

1. PMs manage Project Leads. This includes training on construction activities, providing feedback and communicating information between Project Leads and the larger organization. The PM may have a Senior Project Lead or Project Lead Trainer who assists them.

2. PM is responsible for ensuring proper and timely construction work on our clients' homes as outlined in the **'Scope of Work.'** The scope of work is an agreement between the homeowner and SBP that states what work SBP has agreed to do on the home.

3. PMs are responsible for coordinating any necessary pre-volunteer work, a.k.a. Pre-Construction. Examples of this work are as follows:

   a. If needed, roof repairs are made. Soffit, fascia and/or siding damage is fixed, new exterior doors are installed and new windows are ordered and installed.

   b. The framing is checked for termite damage as well as interior door rough openings are made standard sizes, 82 ½ high.

   c. Rough plumbing is installed and inspected (tub/shower surround is installed).

   d. Rough electrical is installed and inspected. A layout is made.

   e. If a central HVAC unit is being used, it is installed and inspected. The house then goes through a framing, or 'close walls' inspection.

4. PM meets with the homeowner and determines cabinets, floors, and lights and describes more specifically what SBP can provide.

5. PM orders all necessary tools and materials to begin the volunteer friendly stages of construction. They will also be responsible for placing your tool/material deliveries and pickups with the Warehouse.

6. PM schedules times for the cabinet and countertop installation, place work orders to have final electric and plumbing completed, and will order the appliances for the kitchen.

7. PM completes a walkthrough with the homeowner and the Director of Construction.

COMMUNICATION WITH YOUR PM

Project Managers (PMs) are your primary resource. They can provide professional support, training, and serve as a sound board. Communication is a two-way street so it is important to communicate clearly and consistently with your PM. Remember, just because a message is sent, does not mean it was received.

Any questions from the homeowner about the scope the work should be directed to the PM. Please **DO NOT** promise to do any work for your homeowner until is cleared with your PM.

If you have problems with volunteers either not showing up or leaving early or if you have too many or too few, contact your PM. (**DO NOT call the volunteer coordinators** – **this just confuses communication!**)

Below is a list of topics/action items Project Leads typically discuss with their PMs:

1. Project schedule and scope of work – we want to stay on budget and on schedule!!

2. Ordering tools and/or materials for the upcoming construction stages.

3. Questions related to the construction of the project.

4. Reporting an accident/injury on site.

5. Time off requests. Turn in 2 weeks in advance. Do not make travel plans until your request has been approved.

6. Being tardy or absent. Contact your PM as soon as you can and at least 1 hour before your shift is to start. This gives them time to find someone to cover your shift.

7. Managing a challenging volunteer, homeowner, or how to motivate volunteers or offer better training.

8. Other information about SBP.

9. Professional advice or guidance.

Remember the only kind of problem is one we don't talk about. Problems are a good thing and a regular part of any workplace. Your PM is an invaluable resource and mentor; communicate problems to find solutions.

"**Having no problems is the biggest problem of all.**"

~Taiichi Ohno~

Construction Phase Checklist

Scheduled start and completion date:	Scheduled Days to complete:
Actual start and completion date:	Actual Days to complete:

Insulation Checklist	SS Sig	Issues/Tips/Notes
Nailers (aka blocking) installed in corners on the ceilings		
Outlets/light switches not covered and marked with spray paint on floor		
Install insulation with 3/8" staples		
R-30 on ceiling		
R-13 on the walls		
Insulation not compressed (fluff don't stuff) but cut to completely fill the space		
Insulation can go over wires, bhind or on the side of pipes,up to light fixures		
Interior bathroom/utility walls insulated (no other interior walls)		
Tools staged for pick up; Scrap materials bagged and staged for pick up		

I verify the above work was completed. This home ready to move to the next phase of construction and there are no defects or issues.

Site Supervisor   Date   Project Manager   Date

Scheduled start and completion date:	Scheduled Days to complete:
Actual start and completion date:	Actual Days to complete:

Drywall Checklist	SS Sig	Issues/Tips/Notes
All nails or screws removed from studs and joists -- nothing sticking out		
Hung kitchen, bathroom and utility closets first; ceilings and then walls		
Used water resistant Green/Purple boards for bathroom(ceiling &walls) utility Plumbing wall and behind		
Hang bedrooms, living room and hallways and other rooms second; ceilings and then walls		
On walls, drywall hung top row first		
On walls and ceilings, drywall hung perpendicular to the studs/joists		
There are no seams over windows/doors or near corners		
Each piece of drywall is hung so that it begins and ends on the center of stud/joist -- no floaters!!		
Butted seams taggered; factory edges (smooth edges) together whener possible		
Full sheets used whenever possible		
Space was cut out for all pipes, outlets, vents, lights and boxes		
There are 5 screws per stud/joist (not per piece of drywall!)		
All screws have been countersunk		

SBP REGISTRATION & WAIVER FORM

** Please save a tree! Use our online registration at...
SBP.FORMSTACK.COM/FORMS/DAYOFREGISTRATION

First name _____   Email: _____
Last name_____   Phone Number: _____

Age Range: 14-5 _____ 16-17 _____ 18-24 _____ 25-35 _____ 36-55_____ 56-65 _____ 66+_____

Address_____ City: _____
State: _____ Zip: _____

Group Name: _____   *Volunteer Dates:* _____

Signature: _____

Volunteer Participant Liability Release Form (Part 1 of 2)
All volunteers must sign these two (2) forms. Group leaders: please make sure that all members of your group have completed these forms. Anyone under 18 must have a parent's signature. Read before signing, as this constitutes the agreement as a volunteer and the understanding of your working relationship with SBP. Thank you!

Volunteer Participant Liability Release Form *(Please read before signing, as this constitutes the agreement as a volunteer and the understanding of your working relationship with SBP. Please print all information clearly. If you are under 18, please have a parent or guardian sign this agreement ahead of time if they will not be coming with you.)*
I acknowledge and state the following: I have chosen to travel to the work site to perform cleanup/construction work in disaster relief. I understand that this work entails a risk of physical injury and often involves hard physical labor, heavy lifting and other strenuous activity; and that some activities may take place on ladders and building framing other than ground level. I certify that I am in good health and physically able to perform this type of work. I agree that SBP, its employees, or agents have the right to take photographs, videotape, or digital recordings of me. I further consent that my name and identity may be revealed therein or by descriptive text or commentary. I waive any rights, claims, or interest I may have to control the use of my identity or likeness in whatever media used. I understand that there will be no financial or other remuneration for recording me, either for initial or subsequent transmission or playback. In the event that my supervising disaster organization arranges accommodations, I understand that they are not responsible or liable for my personal effects and property and that they will not provide lock up or security for any items. I will hold them harmless in the event of thief or for loss resulting from any source or cause. I further understand that I am to abide by whatever rules and regulations may be in effect for the accommodations at that time. By my signature, for myself, my estate and my heirs, I release, discharge, indemnify and forever hold SBP, together with its officers, agents, servants and employees, harmless from any and all causes of action arising from my participation in this project and

Reflection Questions

1. At your company or organization, are there any sacred cows? Are there instances in which, even with the best intention, you prioritize process (the way you have always done it) over outcomes? Have you dismissed ideas merely saying or thinking, "That is not how we do it"?

2. What role does your identity play? Can you think of instances when good and committed people may be fearful or become uncomfortable doing things a different way?

3. Have you seen instances where outsiders—people from another industry, company, or department—have innovative insights? What allowed them to have these insights? What are some things that you can do on your team to create an environment that is safe for raising and embracing new ideas?

4. Does your company or organization talk about problems? Does everyone agree, or is there a different perception? Why may your company not talk about problems?

5. Are there any aspects related to the creation or mission of your organization that might make it hard to talk about problems? Unlike SBP, is your company populated by long-term professionals? Is it possible that it's harder for people to talk about problems when their identities are tied to their work and excellence?

6. At your organization, are there any well-intended values or phrases that might inhibit the surfacing of problems? The standard for work at SBP was the Grandparent Rule: if the work wouldn't be good enough for your grandparents or loved ones, it had to be redone. We thought that this value would be an asset. Instead, it repressed talking about problems. SBP had a high standard, and the team expected work to be redone. This dulled the expectation of systematic improvement.

7. Are there aspects to your work where, by using the most skilled workers to do the most complicated work, you can add predictability and efficiency? SBP's construction team progressed from the often-held view that residential rehabs are too unpredictable to accurately schedule time lines and completion dates. By using the most-skilled team members to bring each house to a standardized "current state," predictability from that current state was possible.

8. How would you define the ethos of your organization? Do people have any shared identity that shapes decision making?

9. Who would you want to hear from to build that identity? How would you spread it through the organization? Brainstorm a few aspirational identities that would shape decision making in a positive way at your organization.

10. Are you willing to go through a 360 review? Who would you include? Who would run it for you?

11. At your organization, are there any things that you produce (reports, studies, products) that present workflow and scheduling challenges? Are there products that are similar in one way but different in the amount of time that they take to produce? Are you able to control the flow in a way that optimizes predictability for workers and demands/output for customers, whether in-house or market customers?

12. Think of ways that you could level work by volume or by mix. What would be the challenges? What would be the benefits?

13. How would leveling by mix impact employees? Customers?

14. Do things you can't control, like weather, disrupt your production flow?

15. How does this impact your team? The customer?

16. What lessons from the prefab process SBP used could be used to level your flow?

17. How do you on-board new team members? How do you align on culture and ethos? Is your on-boarding consistent or person dependent?

18. Are there any lessons from SBP's evolution that could benefit your organization?

19. How could you use kamishibai, or paper theater, in parts of your organization that are not production based?

About the Authors

Liz McCartney

Liz co-founded SBP in 2006, after spending two weeks with her then boyfriend, Zack, volunteering in New Orleans six months after Hurricane Katrina. Today she is the Executive Director of SBP's New Orleans operation. She leads SBP's ongoing rebuilding work in the city, including the direction of SBP's volunteer management and construction team. She has also led the expansion of SBP's innovative Opportunity Housing program, which redevelops blighted New Orleans properties into affordable homes for first-time low-moderate-income home buyers and generates revenue that is reinvested into SBP's owner-occupied rebuilding program.

In partnership with Toyota, Liz led her team to reduce the average time to rebuild a house from 116 to 61 days. The model used to achieve these results has become SBP's standard construction model, applied to all of the organization's work nationwide.

Liz speaks nationally on a number of topics including disaster recovery and women's leadership. She has delivered addresses at her alma mater, Boston College, and participated on panels at the Farmers Insurance Open Executive Women's Day.

In 2008, Liz was named the CNN Hero of the Year for her innovative work in helping Katrina survivors return home and in 2016 she was nominated as a CNN SuperHero of the Decade for her continued work in disaster recovery in South Louisiana following devastating floods that summer. In recognition of her dedication, Liz has twice been named a White House Champion of Change (2011 and 2013) and in 2011 was awarded an Urban Innovation Fellowship at Tulane University to scale and replicate SBP's model across the country, with support from the university.

Prior to founding SBP, Liz taught middle school in Washington, D.C., and San Francisco. Before that she served with the Peace Corps in Lesotho in southern Africa. She received a B.A. from Boston College, an M.A. from The George Washington University, and an honorary doctoral degree from Muhlenberg College.

Liz and her husband, Zack, live in New Orleans with their son, Jack, and two cats.

Zack Rosenburg

Zack co-founded SBP in 2006 after spending two weeks with his then girlfriend, Liz, volunteering in New Orleans six months after Hurricane Katrina. His realization that a delayed recovery causes extensive human impact and that too many survivors suffer unnecessarily drove SBP's mission of shrinking time between disaster and recovery.

Today, Zack directs the strategic vision, marketing, partnership development, and fundraising for SBP. Following a disaster, he plays a direct role in advising local, state, and federal government officials. He has worked closely with elected officials from South Carolina, New York, and West Virginia, as well as officials at HUD, helping them to craft effective long-term recovery programs.

Innovative SBP programs that Zack has designed include: Opportunity Housing, an innovative blight-eradicating/affordable housing program that turns blighted properties into well-built affordable housing, and Disaster Resilience and Recovery Lab, which shares SBP's learnings, methods, and model with at-risk and disaster-impacted communities.

Zack speaks nationally on a broad array of topics including disaster resilience and recovery policy, organizational culture development, high-impact innovation, and leadership. His work has been featured in *Newsweek, US News and World Report, The Wall Street Journal, The Washington Post*, and Politico (politico.com).

Before founding SBP, Zack was an E. Barrett Prettyman Teaching Fellow at the Georgetown University Law Center and ran an indigent criminal defense practice in Washington, D.C. One of Zack's most meaningful victories was freeing a man who served 23 years for a murder that he did not commit.

For his work, Zack has been recognized as New Orleanian of the Year and Mid-Atlantic Innocence Project Champion of Justice. He has received the Manhattan Institute Social Innovation Award and was also honored as one of 12 recipients from around the world of the 2018 Social Entrepreneurs of the Year Award by the Schwab Foundation for Social Entrepreneurship

Zack received a B.A. from Ohio Wesleyan University and a J.D. from the American University Washington School of Law. He has received an Honorary Doctorate from Muhlenberg College and a distinguished alumnus award from Washington College of Law.

Zack and his wife, Liz, live in New Orleans with their son, Jack, and two cats.

Acknowledgments

We hope that this book is useful to people who can't abide human suffering and inefficiency. We thank our parents and Zack's grandmother and, especially, Liz's mom, Marion, who joined us on the first trip to St. Bernard Parish.

We thank each evolution of SBP AmeriCorps members, the volunteers who keep coming, and the best staff in the NGO world. We thank our Board, who deftly balances our drive for constant improvement with belief in the leadership team with the governance necessary for a group committed to scaled and system-level impact.

We thank Toyota, especially all of the TSSC people, past and present; Jamie Bonini for his leadership at TSSC; Pat Pineda for initially believing in us; Latondra Newton for game-changing investment; and Mike Goss for his unwavering, insightful, and creative support.

We are deeply thankful for the team and leadership at LEI, who saw the value in SBP's story, who provided keen guidance in writing this book, and who put up with our recalcitrance and delay in opening up. We thank Emily Adams for pulling on threads, not showing any frustration, and helping us uncover our voice.

We thank SBP's clients, who continue to inspire us with their dignity, grace, and perseverance when facing an abyss of uncertainty.

In addition to the AmeriCorps members who have engaged with SBP, we would also like to thank those people who in any way support AmeriCorps: those working at Corporation for National Community Service, parents and loved ones of AmeriCorps members, and elected officials who invest in this extraordinarily important American program—one that harnesses the connectedness and commitment of American people to serve, help, and invest to make the world work better for more people. We often find strength during trying times by thinking about the diverse group of AmeriCorps members and the selfless commitment to others that they make.

Finally, we thank our son, Jack, who brings joy, light, and energy to our life and who, through knowing him, makes us work even harder for parents who love their kids just as much.

Index